THINGS
MY
FATHER
TAUGHT
ME

OWEN D. NICHOLS, Ed.D.

TPi.
Transformation Publishing, Inc.
Virginia

TPi

Transformation Publishing, Inc.
George H. Anderson, Publisher
11915 Escalante Court
Reston, VA 20191 USA

Library of Congress Cataloging-in-Publication Data
Nichols, Owen D.
Card Number: 98-065106
Library of Congress
Cataloging-in-Publications Division
101 Independence Avenue, SE
Washington, DC 20540-4320

ISBN 0-9663573-0-2

PRINTED IN THE UNITED STATES OF AMERICA

FRONT COVER: WILLIAM H. NICHOLS, FATHER
OWEN D. NICHOLS, SON

BACK COVER: OWEN D. NICHOLS, ED.D. 1997
PHOTO BY OLAN MILLS

EDITED BY MARGO L. ANDERSON

DEDICATION

This book is dedicated to the memory of my loving mother and father, who were the givers and benefactors of the lives of ten children.

It is also dedicated to my nine brothers and sisters and to my wonderful wife. Although some members of my family have departed from this earth, all of us that remain continue to maintain the oneness that defines family.

MY PRECIOUS MOTHER AND FATHER IN 1957.

MOTHER

Pearl H. Nichols
Born: August 20, 1896
Raleigh, North Carolina
Died: 1971

FATHER

William H. Nichols
Born: November 14, 1890
Raleigh, North Carolina
Died: 1961

INTRODUCTION

My father was not a highly educated man as far as formal education is concerned, but he was educated beyond imagination in the knowledge of life and living. During the early years of my childhood, I was given more direction from my father than I could comprehend at the time. After I grew up and began to think about the things that he had presented to me, I realized that he was really a super teacher.

Whether he knew the depth of his wisdom, I shall never know, but it has become abundantly clear to me that I learned what life was all about from this man who was my father. Although there were many things that he could not have experienced himself, because of the state of the society in which he lived, he was still able to pass along to me enough knowledge and information on the art of living for me to be able to cope with many of the problems that I would later face.

He prepared all of his children to face the realities of life. My father's teachings were manifest during his life, and his lessons continued to assert themselves long after he departed from this earth. As long as his descendants remain, those lessons will be part of our lives and heritage.

In this book, I am expressing the teachings and the thoughts of my father in terms that will convey to the reader the real meaning of his philosophy. Even if this philosophy is not clearly understood from the way it is expressed herein, at least there are inferences and conclusions that are conveyed that will have meaning and relevance to those who ponder their significance.

There is no chronology to this information. Each section is separate unto itself. Each conveys special nuggets of wisdom from this great man. Each has its own intrinsic value that will become more meaningful as you, the reader, bring to mind your own—different and yet similar—experiences.

TO OWEN AND ALL OTHERS WHO SHARE

It gives me great pleasure to introduce the author to you, the reader. The joy and satisfaction that you will experience as each word and each phrase imprints itself upon your mind, and memories of times spent with your father, mother, siblings, and significant others are recognized with humor, joy, sadness and with tenderness toward your own parents and loved ones. The feelings and experiences that rise in your bank of memory will cause you to read this book many times and you will want to share it with other persons as has Owen, in this book. It will hold a warm place in your heart and in your library of must have and must keep items.

Owen D. Nichols is a friend, father, husband, brother, educator and a clear example of a son honoring the memory of his father and mother and so, honors and trusts all of us by sharing an important part of his life and the solid impact that his father had upon him and his siblings. As I continue to read and enjoy "Things My Father Taught Me," I remember my father and his teachings. Despite some differences in style, the lessons are universal. This is a story of every man -- transcending race, gender, ethnicity, culture and time, with an eye toward the future and the expectation that we, their sons and daughters, will have a more fruitful, expansive, family and spiritual life than even they had.

In this work, the author lovingly and without guile, exposes his life story and the story of his family to us in a manner that we can relate to at all class, social and economic levels. The author encourages you to think about the meaning of life, how you carry yourself and interact with other human beings, and how to overcome the high and low points of life. In every chapter of this work we have the opportunity to discover ourselves as men and women and as parents and children. I do not think that I am stretching to say that we have been presented with a level of information which could enhance our ability to deal better with conflict and conflict resolution in our relationships, on our jobs and in our churches and spiritual lives. In the chapter "What Kind Of Christian Are You"?, it reads like unto a sermon which all of us might repeat and ask many questions among which are: what kind of Christian am I?; what kind of person am I?; do I need to change my behavior toward myself and others? These are but a few of the questions that come to me and demand answers in the quiet times of prayer or meditation.

Some of you know and have known Owen for a long time. He is a pleasure to be with and share ideas and philosophies of life. He is a very good story teller and enjoys and presents a good joke. His wife Delores is his constant and faithful companion, they love each other and love their family and friends, they are strong in their faith and are responsible and truthful people. They are also brave, caring, open and live The Gospel of Jesus Christ daily. I am proud to be counted, along with my wife Margo, as a friend and confidant. When you finish reading this wonderful work, you will have similar feelings.

George H. Anderson
Reston, Virginia
January 23, 1998

CONTENTS

1

THE KEYS AND THE GATES

There were many times when my father would sing a song, particularly on Saturday after he had received his pay envelope from the Bursar at Meredith College in Raleigh, North Carolina. This would let me know whether or not he would be financially viable for the weekend and for the coming week. If he sang the song, ***"I've Got The Keys To The Kingdom,"*** it meant that he felt good about his financial condition on that day and was sure that he would be able to take care of all his obligations until the next payday. It meant that he would not have to worry about having to pay the bill collectors who were certain to visit the house sometime between Monday and Friday. He would be prepared to satisfy them. It also meant that he could give my mother enough money to buy food for the family so that hunger would not prevail for the following week. Along with these feelings, he could look forward to providing some recreation and fun activities for the family. I was always very happy to hear the song about the "keys."

I have since decided that he was equating the keys to the kingdom with the ability to conquer, the ability to enter into a situation by which he could control his own destiny, because he was equipped with the keys to compete with the forces of financial need. He felt that he could enter the kingdom of survival with the resources necessary to reside there. He was also saying to me that he was indeed the master of his own fate and that he had no worries at that point in time, neither financial nor otherwise.

On the other hand, if my father sang a song with the long title, "Three Gates In The East, Three Gates In The North, Three Gates In The South and Three Gates In The West, Twelve Gates To The City, Hallelujah," I knew that he was in trouble. This song about the twelve gates to the city was to show me that even though one might be able to enter the city from many directions, that entry was contingent upon some special means that would allow one to pass through the gates. To remain in the city also meant that one must either be able or equipped to control something in that city, using one's own keys. Entering the gates had no real meaning if somewhere in that city there was a property source with doors locked to everyone else except to the owner of the keys. Sometimes my father had the keys and at other times he could get to the door, but had no way to open it.

It was only as an adult that I became aware that both of the two songs my father sang on Saturday were based on passages from the Holy Bible. When he said that he had the keys to the kingdom, there is no question in my mind now that he meant that he was holding the keys to heaven. In the King James Version of the New Testament, Matthew 16:19, the passage reads as follows:

"I will give you the keys of the kingdom of heaven, and whatever you loose on earth shall be loosed in heaven."

Here, my father was equating the possession of sufficient money to do the things necessary to care for himself and his family as no less than owning the keys to the kingdom of heaven, at least until those keys were taken away from him by the loss or expenditure of that money.

Even more obvious to me is the fact that he was referring to the passage in Revelation when he sang about the twelve gates to the city. Revelation 21:10-17 reads:

"And in the Spirit he carried me away to a great, high mountain, and showed me the holy city of Jerusalem coming down out of heaven from God, its radiance like a jasper, clear as crystal. It had a great, high wall, with twelve gates, and at the gates twelve angels, and on the gates the names of the twelve tribes of the sons of Israel were inscribed; on the East three gates, on the North three gates, on the South three gates, and on the West three gates. And the wall of the city had three foundations, and on them the twelve names of the apostles of the Lamb."

The sadness shown by singing the song about the twelve gates manifested itself in the reality that although the city and its' twelve gates were approachable from any direction, my father could not enter the city through even one of the twelve gates. Money was regarded either as the ticket or as the password necessary for admittance into the city of Jerusalem. On those Saturdays when he was incapable of meeting the requirement for entry into the city, he was not blessed with the ticket or with the password.

What he taught by these songs was that man does not always control his own course in life. If one could determine his own course in life, be it on a daily, weekly, monthly, or even on an extended time basis, one would certainly retain the keys to the kingdom that would allow him to enter the chosen city where streets are paved with gold and the fatted calf is always available for feasting. For my father, this was not the case. He was telling me in a clear and easily understood way that I would have to face the same type of situation as I developed into manhood. There would be times when I would be happy and prosperous, and there would be times when the burdens of life could not be lifted without suffering. I could expect to be able to sing at times that I had the keys to the kingdom, but I could also expect to sing about the twelve gates to the city, since there would be times when I would not possess the means by which I could enter that city by using my own resources. Although it may be possible to live free of problems, at times my father was telling me that I would probably not be in a position to live that way always. I had better be aware of the bad times as well as the good times. He was also saying that I should learn how to assess my own situation and make the best plans I could to deal with all situations.

"I FISHES WHERE THEY LETS ME"

My father's grammar was not as bad as the title of this section suggests. For him, fishing was the means through which he relaxed, answered the desire of challenge and developed a sense of self-determination in doing what he wanted when he wanted to do it. He was using the most important recreational activity in his life to get the point across. The message was and the emphasis was, in no uncertain terms, the segregationist and racist nature of the environment in which we lived. My father was telling me in a way that I could understand that conditions for him and for me in North Carolina were different than they were for certain other people. He could not do what he wanted to do where he wanted to do it unless he conformed to the rules of segregation extant at that time. Those rules were very simple. Black people could fish at certain public spaces on the river and creek banks, but they could not fish at the private lakes and pond owned, reserved for and controlled by white people.

Whereas these rules applied, in this case to fishing, there were similar rules that applied to life in general during that day and time. My father, not being a militant or an activist of any kind, wanted me to know that I should be wary of the way that I behaved and not expect to do things when and where I wanted to do them just because I wanted to do them—unless I followed the rules of the day. In this way I would be able to keep out of trouble and I should always keep in mind who I was and know how the rules affected me. In other words, he did not want me to forget that there were some things that I would be unable to obtain because of the color of my skin.

Time played a favorable role in helping me realize that my father was not willing to buck the system that "let him fish where they would allow him to fish." Within a very short time after he told me about this situation, I began to question him about race relations in Raleigh. He was to a great extent wedded to the notion that things were not too bad, as long as we were able to keep the peace and not be harmed bodily.

As a young upstart, I made him feel very uncomfortable with my questions, since my questions always contained implied answers. I could not comprehend the rules that required me to walk past several public schools each day and not be permitted to enter them as a student. I was "going to school" at the same time and just as the white kids were "going to school." I could not understand why I had to drink water from a special fountain labeled "Colored" in the various public places in Raleigh, such as the department stores, the museum and the zoo. Riding on the back of the bus never did make sense to me. I did not know why I could not sit anywhere I wanted to sit. The fact that the bus station and the train station had separate areas for black riders and white riders seemed like a terrible waste, so I raised questions about these things.

My father had no acceptable answers to my many questions. He tried to impress upon me that I should accept the truth of time, and time in this case was such that whatever transpired in my life at any given moment was affected and even controlled by the norms of society. For me that society was hostile, but my father felt that I would face more hostility if I were to attack the rules of the day.

Fortunately, even before my father died, there was some easing of the rules. He began to see that one doesn't always have to accept the rules of another just because those rules exist. Also there are options available when someone else's rules are not fairly drawn. In many instances, these rules may represent a detriment to the well-being of all, or at least some of those who are expected to abide by them. I was not happy with this part of my father's teaching. I feel that I contributed to his own learning, letting him know in a respectful way that just as time is not static, neither must the condition placed upon us by time be static.

Segregation in Raleigh, North Carolina in the late 1930's and early 1940's when I was growing up was as real as life itself. There was nothing that my father could teach or tell me to change that. His awareness of the situation, however, was depicted in his pattern of acceptance, not unusual to that time. He would try to make me see what was happening by telling me to be quiet and accept what he knew was wrong. He did not

think that he had any means by which to fight the
system. What I really believe my father was trying to
point out to me was that he felt that segregation could
be practiced without racism being practiced at the same
time. My belief was, and is, that segregation is based
on racism, and had there been no racism, there would
have been no segregation. He never faltered in his
acceptance probably because he believed that God had
decided how life was to be lived, and he was not about
to tamper with God's plan.

An interesting incident that had a measurable effect
upon my father, took place at the Trailways Bus Station
in Raleigh early in the 1950's. It involved one of my
brothers who was in the United States Army at the time.
This brother was fair-skinned and could easily be
mistaken for a white person if no attention was paid to
his hair. He had come home on furlough and was now
ready to return to Fort Bragg, North Carolina where he
was stationed. My father had taken him to the bus
station and returned home. As things turned out, my
brother had forgotten something that he should have
taken with him and telephoned my father from the bus
station to ask him to bring the forgotten object to him
before the bus took off. My father was obliging and
asked me to come with him to the bus station. Evidently,
my father and I arrived at the station sooner than my
brother had anticipated. This appeared to be the case,
because we did not find him in the "colored" section of
the station. Rather, we found him in the "white" section,
sitting at the snack bar eating a hot dog and drinking a
soda. When he saw us entering the "white" section, he
began gesturing to us with great animation to go back
outside and not approach him. What he had done was
to pull his cap far enough over his hair so that it was

not visible. Thus, he looked just as white as any white person in the station. He did not want my father and me to blow his cover. He was taking advantage of the better accommodations provided for white people.

My brother's action was to me one of the funniest things I had ever seen him do, and I got a great charge out of it. My father, however, did not find what he had done to be funny at all. Instead, he became very nervous over the incident and admonished my brother for having done what he did. This was just another example of my father's acceptance of what was.

Out of respect for my father, I did not get involved in activities that were certain to embarrass him. Although I would have liked to participate in programs that challenged the segregationist and racist nature of life in Raleigh at the time of my rearing, there was not enough of an incentive from others to cause me to consider going against the will of my father. I must believe that most other children of that day were taught to hold the same kind of respect for, and allegiance to, the older generation as that which my brothers, sisters and I had for our parents. The world of today is such that many children do not practice the kind of parental reverence that I knew. Family cohesiveness and stability have been relegated to a level of secondary importance, and as a result, parents do not seem to have the great influencing power over children that they once had. Of course, the attitudes and behavior of parents now may not be the same as they were then.

Parent/child relationships have suffered from forces that tend to suggest that independent living is better than interdependent living. Unlike the position taken by my father, and certainly by my mother, family life and family ties do not appear to be as precious and cherished as they once were. The keys to the kingdom that my father always sought may have involved far more important things to him than simply entering a city where tangible riches represented the utmost. I believe he also saw the city as a place where family love abides and the houses are filled with furnishings— such as the virtues of caring and sharing. As important as the existence of golden streets was, if the pedestrians on these streets of gold possessed cold hearts, the gold was of no value.

Apparently my father did not choose to use his life and time to worry about segregation and racism. He had other things to concentrate on requiring the use of his energies. Once he had explained what segregation was all about, he had no need to discuss it anymore. Little did he realize though that those other things, whatever they might have been, were often made more difficult to handle as a direct result of segregation and racism.

"I fishes where they lets me" was not the grammar of my father, but it was ingrained in his awareness of segregation as a fact of life.

HE LIKES MEN AND NEEDS TO BE WATCHED

There was a certain man who was friendlier toward the boys in my neighborhood than were other men. I would ask my father why all of the people could not be like this man. I must have been all of eight years old, but this question gave my father an opportunity to tell me about homosexuality and the odd behavior of this man who was so kind to the boys.

My father started by telling me that the man liked other men and needed to be watched. He also told me that this man liked boys in the wrong way. He told me to stay away from the man because he may try to do something to me that would be improper. With my young inquisitive mind, I wanted to know what the man might do and why he liked men and boys better than he liked women and girls. My father was really at a loss for an explanation that he thought I could understand, so he simply told me that I had plenty of time to find out what he termed "queer people" do to each other. Needless to say, I kept my distance from the man in question, but studied his behavior as much as I could.

One day my father and several of his friends were discussing a fishing trip. The man who liked men apparently wanted to go on the trip. I overheard one of the men say that this person had offered to pay all of his expenses for the trip if he were allowed to join the group. What a laugh the person relating this information got from the others when he told them what had been offered. The friends of my father said that if the "queer person" were to go on the trip, only the two of them would go. Apparently, the men did not want to include the "queer" and therefore threatened to call the whole thing off unless it was made clear that he could not go.

To me, this encounter was even more meaningful than the original statement my father had made concerning a man liking men. I learned that people have serious differences, but each has a right to practice and express those differences. The men who were going on the fishing trip did not agree with the practices of the person who wanted to join them, so they expressed their differences from him by denying him the privilege of associating with them. This was indeed an exercise of their right to decide with whom they chose to spend their time, but it was also an expression of condemnation directed toward the person whose sexual preferences differed from their own. The rigidity with which known homosexuals were kept in isolation from the mainstream was a reflection of prejudice and weakness in standing up for the rights of the one who was different.

What I really could not understand was why the "queer person" represented a threat to any of the others who wanted to go on the trip. Why was he so strong that he could make someone else do something that was undesirable and unwanted? Here was a lesson in the behavior of people as well as in the strength of individuals.

The conclusion that I now draw from my father's teaching with regard to the "queer person" is that he wanted me to learn how to deal with unusual situations. Some situations might be familiar, but others that I might face somewhere along the line in life, could be harmful to my own way of life. Yet he also wanted me to know that I should not be influenced by the desires of others in making decisions of my own. This lesson was very helpful to me during my high school years. To my dismay, I learned that several of my high school male teachers were homosexual. My schoolmates would tell me stories about certain teachers approaching them and asking them to perform sexual acts with them. At least one of the teachers would give money to the boys and buy gifts for them. He would lure the boys to his house and take advantage of them in an abusive manner. He would also inflate the boys' grades who were a part of his game. Fortunately for me, my father had alerted me to the likes of such people, and I was able to avoid getting involved with any of them.

Those teachers who participated in sexual abuse of boys in my high school had no compunctions about being unfair to the boys who refused to cooperate with them. When I was in the ninth grade, there was a prize to be given to the student who had the highest academic average at the end of the school year. Since numerical grades—not letter grades—were given, it was easy to determine who had the highest average. My average had been computed as the highest, but when one of the persons who taught ninth-grade English, and who also was one of the male student abusers, learned that none of his boys held the top grades, he changed the grade of one of his students in an effort to bring his overall average above mine. Even after giving this student a grade of one hundred for the English course taught by the homosexual teacher, my academic average for the year was still best. The excuse used by the homosexual teacher for changing the grade of the other student was that he had made a mistake in reporting the grade.

This experience taught me such an alarming lesson in dishonesty—in the actions of the English teacher—I could never develop any respect for him. My father's early warning about certain people who needed to be watched was crystal clear as I went through my high school years.

PREPARE FOR SUNDAY ON SATURDAY

The church and religion were extremely important to my father. He had a rather strange way of teaching his children what the church and religion were all about. Each Saturday evening, he would go through a ritual, whereby he would fill in the blank spaces on his church envelopes, showing his name and the amount of money that he was giving for the regular collection and for the building fund. In most instances, he would give seventy-five cents for the regular offering and twenty-five cents for the building fund. Having made somewhere between eight and twelve dollars for the week, he was giving between eight and one-half and twelve and one-half percent of his salary to the church. On an average, this meant that he was tithing at the level of ten percent of his earnings.

He would be enthusiastic about his giving, not

because he wanted his children to look up to him for doing so, but because he wanted his children to develop the same kind of commitment that led him to give so generously in the first place. He knew that if the act of giving to the church made him feel so good that he could "brag" about it, that same type of feeling would be developed in the minds of his children.

I was very much impressed by the Saturday ritual and tried to give from the few cents I was able to acquire, at the same level at which my father was giving. As I grew older, I discovered that this part of his teaching was not as effective, even though I continued to give as generously as I could. The desire to tithe has always been with me, but I have not always made the choice to practice a full tithe. Neither have my brothers and sisters.

Money was not the only thing that my father gave generously to the church. He also gave as much of his time and talents as he could manage. He participated in an adult Sunday School class each week, and he served as an usher. He took great pride in being able to show people where to sit and in collecting their envelopes and cash contributions for the church. Many physical chores, such as painting and plastering, were done by him whenever there was a need for such. He considered this type of service to the church as even more important than the money he gave. One reason for this belief was that he knew the church would have to pay more for the service if it had to be purchased. The value for the service was much greater than the amount of money he could contribute. Thus, he was tithing far more than the average ten percent of his earnings given in the envelope. He was tithing an amount of time and energy in the form of service that defied quantification.

My father shared his feelings about church and religion through many discussions with his children. He would raise very interesting questions about fear and the devil. He would sometimes cause us to become frightened by the thought that the devil would come to us and do us harm. Once he knew that we were frightened, he would then talk about how God is able to protect those who have the faith and who believe that the devil is no match for God. The funny thing about these discussions is that they seemingly would always take place on Saturday. I do believe that my father felt that if he could instill into our minds certain thoughts about religion near the day the formal church services were held, we would be better prepared to participate in the services and would get more from them than we otherwise might have gotten. He knew that young minds needed to be prompted, challenged, stimulated and steered if the proper attitudes about the church and religion were to be developed therein.

He taught all of his children about religion by example. The teaching and the examples were so strong that each of us followed in his footsteps as far as the church is concerned, particularly with respect to giving of our time, talents and presence.

The importance of Saturday, among other things, was to prepare for Sunday. For me, it still is.

MAN IS MESSING UP OUR FOOD

One of the most startling revelations I experienced as I studied and majored in chemistry, both at the undergraduate and graduate levels of college, was that my father had been so knowledgeable about the effects of so many chemicals on the human body. He was very much distressed over the use of potent fertilizers and pesticides used to increase the size and quantity of vegetables and fruits grown and to protect them from being eaten by insects. He was even more concerned that the chemically-laced feed given to farm animals to make them grow faster and larger was detrimental to the health of the human consumer.

It is now clear to me that my father was, in fact, a naturalist of the first kind. He did not want his food to be contaminated with anything that did not come from natural growth.

His love of fishing was coupled by his love for fish as a source of food. He felt that the water was the best place for food to be grown and that man would have a harder time fouling up the food that comes from the water than he would in fouling up the food that comes from the soil or from the flesh of animals. My father did not realize that man is not only capable of contaminating the water, but also that he had already begun (even during my father's time) to pollute the rivers and streams, as well as the seas and the oceans. What a disappointment it would have been for him to discover that the fish he caught could have been chemically unclean. In spite of his limited knowledge, he had faith that food produced in a natural environment was different and better for the human body than the food produced through artificial means.

Ironically, the make-up of my human system proves my father's point of view. I am personally affected by the use of certain chemicals in food. Although my problem is different from the problems pointed out by my father, it is still a chemical problem. When the widely used chemical, monosodium glutamate (MSG), is present in anything that I eat, I am wiped out for twenty to twenty-four hours. If I eat anything with sodium nitrite in it, my eyes become affected, and I have difficulty seeing for an hour or two. There are several other chemicals that I have isolated as enemies to my own well-being. As I think of the problems I have with various chemicals, I become increasingly aware of the wisdom of my father and the message he conveyed to me that "man is messing up our food."

Poultry producers sometimes boast that they can grow chickens so efficiently that for every pound of feed the chicken eats, a pound of weight results in the chicken. This pound-for-pound production is truly wonderful as far as the marketing of chickens is concerned, but it is without question, a manifestation of unnatural growth. Is it possible that chicken meat can taste the same coming from this process as it would if the growth were natural? I can recall that chicken was never so fatty in the distant past as it is today. I can also recall the time that chicken had a standard color. But no more. Chicken now comes in almost any shade of yellow, beige, white or off-white that one desires. If my father thought that man was "messing up our food" during his day, he would be appalled to know what is happening to food today. Not only is man altering our food, but man is also producing unnatural food. Even if food is all right when it is produced, more times than not, some artificial seasoning or material to keep it from sticking to the pan will be used to mess it up anyway.

My father's concern for chemical contamination of food was extended beyond just that of adding substances or using pesticides and fertilizers to make things grow better-faster-larger. He also was very concerned about the handling of food as it was being prepared. Was the raw food washed properly? Were the pans and stirring or cutting utensils clean? Was the food cooked long enough to be sure that any bacteria that might have been in it were destroyed by heat? These are the kinds of questions raised by him in connection with food preparation. Admittedly, some of his children, including myself, probably go to the extreme in watching what is ingested. Sanitary handling of food is an absolute necessity if we are to consume it. This places a severe limitation on the way we eat and the places where we eat, but we try to be sure that all the rules of sanitation are followed before we eat.

An interesting experience with food occurred one time when my immediate family was visiting relatives in Roanoke Rapids, North Carolina. These were relatives on my mother's side who were very dear to us, and the whole family trusted our wonderful elderly cousin who had cooked what appeared to be a delicious meal. However, my family did not eat the food on that day because we observed too many flies flying around the house. Surely, we thought, some of the flies had come in contact with the food and if that was the case, it was unfit to eat. This decision was borne out completely when the lady of the house vigorously swished a cardboard fan across a dark cake that suddenly became white. The cake appeared to have been covered with raisins, but it turns out that the cake was covered with flies. One of my sisters had thought that the cake was chocolate, but that too was an incorrect observation. The cake situation vindicated my family's decision to refrain from eating any of the food. If there had been any question about the wisdom of that decision, it was resolved when we learned that the raisins were really flies.

My youngest sister was the only one of the ten children in our family who was not born at home with the assistance of a midwife. When she was born, my mother, for the first time, was in the hospital for the delivery. While my mother was away, my father, feeling very good about the new baby, decided that he would cook for the other children, instead of having one of my older sisters do the cooking. He prepared what we considered to be an elaborate meal of fried chicken, mashed potatoes, string beans, homemade biscuits and fresh fruit for dessert. He was most proud that he had purchased a live chicken, killed it, picked it and prepared it for cooking himself. He knew that the chicken was as fresh as it could possibly be. Everything was great until we sat down at the table and one of my sisters found a chicken feather in a biscuit. This upset her so that she not only refused to eat the food that day, but she has refused to eat homemade biscuits from that day to the present. She says that she will never again eat homemade biscuits. She even refuses to cook them herself.

There is certainly no member of my family today who is as finicky about eating as is this sister mentioned above. If she does not feel within herself that whatever food placed before her has been handled and prepared with an absolute commitment to cleanliness, no matter how good it may look or taste, she will not touch it. When she cooks herself, there is never any doubt about the antiseptic and clinical quality of her food.

This food-finicky sister has always imposed strict rules upon anyone who uses her kitchen sink. The washing of hands in her kitchen sink is prohibited. Although dirty dishes and pans may be rinsed in the sink, apparently she feels that the dirt from one's hands will have a contaminating effect upon the surface of the sink, and therefore she bans hand-washing.

Another sister, the youngest, has twin kitchen sinks. She designates one in which hands may be washed, while the other is maintained exclusively for the rinsing or washing of dirty pans and dishes. There is obvious influence by the older sister on the younger sister in this attention to cleanliness.

My father's concerns for what was happening to food during his lifetime were completely valid. Most people today have to depend upon commercial sources for food products and have limited ability to do anything about the problem. My father wisely taught us to be aware of contaminants in food. Today, if he were alive, he would likely be a strong proponent of organic food and of attention to cleanliness in the preparation of all foods.

THIS A PICTURE OF MY FATHER ON SUNDAY AFTERNOON. WHAT THE PICTURE CONFIRMS IS THAT HE REFUSED TO DRESS CASUALLY AT ANY TIME OF DAY ON SUNDAY.

THERE'S FLOUR THERE

One of the great lessons taught by my father came from his response to my mother during a serious discussion of what she was going to cook for dinner one day. She had not been able to put together a meal, simply because she did not have anything in the house to prepare. She kept saying to my father that we were going to have to go hungry that day. Having no money with which to purchase food, he finally said to her, "There's flour there."

My mother's reaction to this answer was to go to the kitchen and prepare several bakery-type dishes that required flour as the basic component. Although the family did not have a balanced meal on that day, the family did not go hungry.

To me, a basic lesson in subsistence and survival had come from the statement that my father had made.

One must use that which is available in order to avoid failure and hardship. Even today, my surviving sisters and I refer often to the statement, "There's flour there." We know there is a very special meaning in those words, and the mere mention of them gives us a warm and victorious feeling.

In dealing with our own children, all of us use the essence of the statement in explaining to them that the fundamental means of survival in life often comes from the ability of one to make something happen from one's own resources, irrespective of the meagerness of those resources. The lesson was for my mother, as well as for the children of the family. Following this utterance, she began to see her own resourcefulness in a different light.

There was another time when one of my sisters desperately needed a pair of shoes. No money was available to buy them. Without pressing my father to find the money somewhere, my mother decided that she would make a pair of shoes for my sister. To the amazement of the whole family, she took an old leather pocketbook and cut it up into pieces to form two shoes. She stitched together the pieces by hand and put heavy pieces of cardboard inside the bottoms to reinforce the soles. These handmade shoes served my sister well until my father was able to buy her a pair from the store. My sister wore the shoes to school, and I never heard her complain about other children laughing about them. My mother's ingenuity and resourcefulness had been assisted greatly by the earlier response, "There's flour there."

The flour statement was one of the keys to developing my own sense of values. It also has helped me to teach my children the meaning of a personal value system. It is essential for us to consider spiritual, social, humanitarian and other factors, as well as material resources, in building values. Of greatest importance to me in setting up a value system is whether or not someone else will benefit from it. Self-centered values are in conflict with the value system that I believe all people should strive to maintain. Those who develop (or set) values based upon economic factors lack a critical element of those who are interested in bettering the social and spiritual lives of human beings. An exchange system for products has limited use or meaning and should not be confused with the value of life—the greatest of all values.

HUMOR COMES IN MANY FORMS

The key to family security may rest, to a great extent, on the level of laughter and humor in which the family engages itself. My father taught his family the importance of fun and laughter by being a practical joker and a teller of stories designed to guide our minds away from the troubles of the world. He would never miss the opportunity to make us laugh. There were times when the family would sit together and listen to stories and jokes and laugh so hard that tears would flood our eyes. There are times now when one of my sisters will call me on the telephone or I will call one of them, and we will spend several minutes laughing about a joke, a statement or an event that took place in the past with tears flowing freely. All of my brothers and I seem to have inherited the practical joker role from my father. My own children have also developed a full appreciation for the value of laughter as essential to the family, because of the penchant I have for making them laugh in situations that might otherwise be filled with tension.

One of my brothers worked as a grocery delivery boy when he was in high school, and he decided that he was going to play a joke on my father. He used an item he had bought from the store at which he worked—a pair of bright red wax lips that kids used for chewing. The lips were sugar-filled and gave the chewer a sweet taste, just like chewing gum.

On this particular night, my brother brought the lips home and asked all of us—brothers, sisters and my mother—to help him with the joke. He said that he wanted to make my father think that the lips were his own and that they had gotten red from a fight. My mother suggested that the lights be cut down to a minimum so that my father could not see very well when he came in contact with my brother.

Sure enough, when my father came home, my mother greeted him in agony with the announcement that my brother had been in a terrible fight and looked awful. As he approached my brother, bright red wax lips in place, my father almost passed out as he stood there in disbelief. Finally, after several minutes, my brother removed the wax lips from his mouth and the family laughed about the incident for the rest of the night.

My father did not get angry with my brother, because he knew that if he ever had the opportunity, he would have done the same thing. He would have jumped at it. After this incident, there were absolutely no arguments or conflicts in the family the rest of the night. The only thing anybody wanted to talk about was the red wax lips.

Another incident involving a trip to Neuse River, the closest river to Raleigh, my home town, gave me an opportunity to play a joke on my father. At the time, I was sixteen years old and had just learned to drive a car. My father, along with three of his fishing buddies, had driven to the river to fish. Since my father always parked at the same place, I knew where his car would be located. I persuaded a friend to let me drive his car to the river. When I got there, sure enough, my father's car was parked in its usual spot. I wrote a note that read as follows, "You are in violation of the Game Laws of the state of North Carolina and must appear before the State Court tomorrow morning at 9:00 a.m. to answer charges brought against you by the Game Warden. You are also illegally parked and must defend this act as well." I signed the note, "State Game Warden," and placed it under the windshield wiper on his car.

When my father arrived home, he was distraught. He told my mother that he was in trouble and may have to go to jail. Having alerted my mother to what I had done, she went along with the joke and bemoaned the situation with him. After about two hours of sheer agony, I confessed that I had written the note and told him that he did not have to go to court the next morning at all. The relief he felt was so great that he did not even think of punishing me for playing such a harsh joke on him.

When my own children were young and at home, the dinner table was the most important place for laughter. Very often, when I would catch one of the children looking directly at me, I would open my mouth and show one of them chewed-up food. Naturally, he or she, whichever one it was, would start laughing. My wife would then start questioning the child as to why he or she was laughing so hard, and the act would be disclosed.

I would always deny having done what the child said I did because that would be so improper. Although my wife knew that I was capable of doing what the child had accused me of doing, she was never quite sure what I had done because of the look of innocence she always got from me. After a time, she decided that I was showing the children chewed up food, but she learned to accept it. The kids began to do the same thing to me whenever they got the chance—always avoiding being caught by their mother.

Until this very day, I do not yet know whether our son was playing a joke on my wife and me on one particular day. At the dinner table he made us laugh so hard that we had difficulty finishing our meal. He was about eight years old. That day he had been playing with several balls after school in an open field across the street from the house in which we lived. He had used a baseball, a football and a tennis ball. All of a sudden, he said to me, "Daddy, I lost my balls today." My mind was immediately directed to his genitals, not even thinking of the balls about which he was speaking. This caused the laughter and tears to flow so freely that I was almost completely wiped out. My wife joined in the laughter, along with our three-year-old daughter. Fortunately, our daughter had no idea what we were laughing about, but she got as much out of it as did my wife and I, simply because it was laughter.

One day, perhaps, our son will confess that he was trying to bring laughter to the table rather than simply making an innocent statement that could be interpreted in more than one way. If he was trying to bring laughter to the table, it proves that the love of humor by my father does not stop with his own children. It has transcended at least another generation. Hopefully, that love will never die.

Two incidents with which I was involved a few years ago are a direct result of the humor-filled mind that my father left me. During the time I lived in a Northeast neighborhood in Washington, DC, I always put forth a conscious effort to make people in the community laugh. On one occasion, I designed a petition for members of the community to sign to support me in obtaining a mule and keeping it in my back yard. I took the document to a number of households and explained that I wanted to get the mule so that he could be used to eat the grass in my back and front yards, thereby relieving me of the responsibility of mowing the lawns. I also offered the use of the mule to all who signed the petition so that they too could eliminate the need to cut grass. The petition was such a hit with the neighbors, that every one of them signed it, and for many months the subject was brought up in various community settings, always bringing laughter and fun to the group involved.

The other incident involved only the elderly couple who lived next door to my wife and me. They were avid fans of the Ted Mack Show that aired on television each Sunday evening. The Ted Mack Show was really a talent show, or talent contest that provided an opportunity for amateurs to perform on national television. I informed the couple that I had been selected to appear on the Ted Mack Show. On a given Sunday afternoon in early winter, I dressed myself in heavy clothing, picked up an empty suitcase and went next door to bid good-bye to the couple, because I was headed for New York to perform on the show. I told them that

I would be singing and asked for their blessings and support. They believed me at first and did seriously offer their congratulations. They said that their prayers would be with me for my success in winning. With suitcase in hand, I returned home. My wife called by phone to tell the folk that I was just joking and would not be on the Ted Mack Show that night. They enjoyed the prank so much that both of them talked about it for many years, always getting a new thrill out of the incident each time it was mentioned.

My father would have enjoyed doing the same things I did with the neighbors. His sense of humor was felt well beyond the confines of his own home and appreciated by far more people than his own family. In his opinion, laughter not only keeps families together, it can even keep communities together.

BE SURE YOU ARE RIGHT, THEN MOVE AHEAD

The above statement was made by my father, oh so many times. More than cautiousness was inherent in the comment. However, I never accepted the instruction as a valid means of getting ahead and would challenge him every time I heard it. On one level he was saying to me that I should not consummate any undertaking until I knew for sure that the undertaking was correct. My response at that level was to say to him that I feel chances must be taken sometimes because I could not always know for certain what the results would be. I admitted that, if I could be absolutely sure of what I was doing all the time, I would never have to worry about failure. I would also tell him that if I never faced failure, I would have missed a part of my upbringing.

He never backed off, which suggests that he had gotten a message across to me in a devious kind of way at a different level. Upon reflection, I realize that he might have been telling me to do just what I was determined to do. That is, analyze every aspect of every situation possible to identify, and decide if I am right. If I am, at that point, I should move ahead because I would then know as much about the matter as I could. My rejection of his statement might have been exactly what my father wanted from me. Wisdom is not always obvious to the unwise or even to the uninitiated.

The passage of time has given me an even greater depth of understanding of what he was trying to tell me. As I pursued a career as a research chemist and found myself involved in many very sensitive and sometimes dangerous laboratory operations, I had to know whether things were correct before proceeding. This was essential, since there were times when taking a chance was not safe. Although my father was absolute in his statement about being sure I was right before moving ahead, I do believe that he would now accept my interpretation of the advice. He would even agree that he had been completely successful in guiding me in the direction that he wanted to see me go.

The information may have become more apparent to me as I left the chemistry lab and became an administrator. All too often there is the tendency to look at administrative problems from too narrow a perspective, but with the statement of my father lurking in my mind and the discipline learned in the laboratory, I would always look at problems from as many different perspectives as I could identify. In this way, I felt that my decisions were made on the basis of knowing that I was right before going ahead. Albeit, this may not have been the case, there was a sense of satisfaction present for having looked ahead before moving ahead.

DELIVER US FROM EVIL

My father always worried about the problems of the world, particularly about the spread of evil among humankind. Somehow, I continue to share those worries and deep concerns. I submit that the problems of the world may very well be grounded in the spread of evil. One thing is certain, evil is no less common today and no less wrong today than it was during the lifetime of my father. In fact, evil may be more of a problem today than it was while he lived.

It appears to me that human behavior has become increasingly altered with time—altered in the sense that much of what was considered to be morally wrong, or evil, in the past, has now become either morally right, or is of no moral concern or consequence. This leads me to believe that many people have begun to cover up evil under the guise of contemporary morality. This may be another way of saying that old fashioned "sin" is no longer wrong, and therefore, people do not need to worry about it anymore. But I say that sin, either old fashioned or modern, is a manifestation of evil and will always be morally wrong.

If we go back to the very beginning of human existence on earth, we learn that Satan introduces Adam and Eve to evil in the Garden of Eden. When the devil coaxed Eve into eating the forbidden fruit, and she, in turn, enticed Adam to eat the same fruit, evil became a part of the human experience. God had just made human life in the form of man and woman. As soon as Adam and Eve were created, the perpetrator of evil, the devil himself, arrived on the scene at almost the same time. The devil has been around a long time, and so has evil.

The story is sometimes told about Moses bargaining with God on the mountain top, supposedly to get God to reduce the number of Commandments. Apparently God started out with twenty-five commandments, but the best Moses could do was to get Him to cut the number to ten. When Moses came off the mountain and reported to his friends, he said that God had indeed been reasonable as far as the number was concerned. However, He held on to the toughest ten of the twenty-five. God felt so strongly about the final ten that He would not write them on paper. Instead, He carved them on tablets of stone so that Moses could not claim that he forgot them. In other words, God was serious about this matter and did not want any foolishness out of Moses.

If one thinks about the Ten Commandments with the seriousness intended by God, and then considers the violation of these Commandments as acts of evil, then one must conclude that the violation of the Ten Commandments is today as it was when God presented them to Moses. When God inscribed such words as, "Thou shalt not kill...steal...commit adultery...bear false witness," He placed no expiration date on any of those directives. I do not believe that God ever intended to allow human beings to reduce, rewrite, or reinterpret His Commandments in such a way that it would be acceptable to break any of them. Yet, many people today fail to take God's Commandments seriously. They have convinced themselves that they have done nothing wrong when they break God's laws by engaging in the practice of evil. Just as my father taught me to be concerned about evil when I was a child, I am equally concerned as an adult.

When Jesus taught us to pray the Lord's Prayer, He was telling us how to communicate with the Father in Heaven. He used the phrase, "Deliver us from evil," as a specific request that we should make to the Father. Not only does this suggest that we already have had some association with evil, but it also is recognition of the power of God to take us away from evil. Interestingly, Jesus did not instruct us to ask God to help us to confront evil; rather, He suggested that we seek deliverance from evil. Now, I believe that God can and does use many different means by which to deliver us from evil. One of those means may very well be deliverance through confrontation, therefore leading to the destruction of evil. Jesus may also have been using a parabolic phrase in teaching us to ask God to deliver us from evil.

Certainly, there are other ways for us to be delivered from evil by God. One way is for God to help us perform acts of goodness in the face of evil. Every time we do something that is pleasing to God, we will have avoided doing something that is evil in His sight. God also delivers us from evil by instilling in our minds and in our hearts the feeling of joy and happiness that comes from serving Him and from concentrating upon the love of His Son, Jesus Christ. When we focus our minds on the beauty of Christian love, evil is squeezed out, and surely we are delivered away from that evil when Christian love abounds. Another way that God delivers us from evil is by establishing situations for us in which we can lose ourselves in the wonderment of Jesus. God gives us the opportunity to join hands with Jesus, and to follow the example of His goodness. The way of Jesus is the antithesis of evil and our way can and should be patterned in the same mode. Evil can be forced out of our lives, with no chance of its survival, if we accept the ways of Jesus and adhere to them. In other words, God gives us the privilege of delivering ourselves from evil.

Quite well known is the Biblical story of Noah and the Ark, which deals with the survival of living creatures. If Noah had not found grace and favor in the eyes of God, in all likelihood, there would be no human life on earth today. According to the book of Genesis, during the time of Noah, God had decided to destroy man—the very creature He had created—because He felt the wickedness and evils of man were too great for man to remain as a part of the universe. God characterized man in a frightful way when He indicated, "...that every imagination of the thoughts of his heart was only evil continually." [Genesis 6:5] If God felt so strongly about the evil in man's heart then, it is quite possible that He feels equally strong about man's behavior today. If man does not, in this day, rid himself of his evil and wicked ways forthwith, it is possible or even probable that God will again take things into His own hands and use His enormous power to bring man back to a state of morality which God Himself can support and condone.

There are those who will remember the very popular radio program of many years ago called, "The Shadow." Before television took over as the preferred form of home entertainment, I dare say that few people with radios failed to listen to the show on Sunday afternoons. My father loved it! I can recall that my whole family would gather around the radio almost ritualistically to hear "The Shadow." The thing I remember most is the ever haunting question and answer that were always presented on the show.

The Question: "Who knows what evil lurks in the hearts of men?"

The Answer: "The Shadow knows."
What is significant about this exchange of question and answer is that there is a profoundness here that might not have been immediately known to the listeners. In reality, the shadow cast by an individual is peculiar, or unique, to that individual, and is a reflection of the inner person and of the outer person. One's shadow may very well know what evil lurks in one's heart, in one's mind, in one's body and even in one's soul. The shadow is an integral and intimate part of one's being that cannot be separated or taken away. There is more to this business of the shadow knowing what evil lurks in the hearts of men than just a catchy response to a radio question. If shadows could readily reveal what evil actually lurks in people's hearts, there would be many people in trouble. It may be, however, that God looks at our shadows and sees what evil is there.

Someone once wrote words to this effect, "When evil

becomes indistinguishable from good, the world is then in a precarious state." Indeed, the world may be approaching the point where the identification of evil is hidden in the lack of concern for evil acts. When little or no concern is given to such expressions of evil as crime and violence, selling harmful drugs to children, abusing children, ignoring the problems of hunger and seeking catharsis through aggressive and dangerous driving, an extremely disturbing question arises as to whether or not evil is looked upon any differently from the way that good is looked upon. Can good and evil be one and the same in the minds of some? It is quite possible.

When the words of George Bernard Shaw are contemplated—namely, "The greatest of evils and the worst of crimes is poverty"—my father's situation, were he still alive, must be considered. He would be well over one hundred years old. He would also be poor and would have to face the ugliness of poverty. Thus, evil would have been created for my father as a result of the creation of poverty. How would he have been delivered from that evil? I believe that the answer rests in the hand and the vision of Jesus Christ, the Son of God. My father accepted Jesus with a humble and contrite heart. In this way, he felt that he could set the stage for the reduction, if not the elimination of evil from his own life. He felt that for every evil thought banished from his mind, there was an equivalent good thought to take its place. He took the position that holding God's hand through His Son, Jesus, would contribute to the eradication of evil. Realizing the greatness of Jesus and becoming enraptured in the honor, glory and praise of the Almighty God, would be the best way to avoid the contamination of evil. If he allowed Jesus to touch him, to talk with him, to guide him, and to maintain contact with him, my father knew that evil could and would be overcome. In simple terms, my father dealt with evil through faith and trust in God. He believed that God would take care of him wherever he was and in whatever he did. He felt that faith had continually delivered him from evil.

DO EVERYTHING YOU CAN FOR OTHERS AND

SOME OF THEM WILL DO FOR YOU

Usually during the month of July, while my father was still working as a custodian and handy man at Meredith College, he would begin gathering various materials from which he could make Christmas gifts for certain designated people at the college. He collected cedar, oak and pine lumber, along with electrical fixtures and an assortment of metal pipes, small pieces of sheet metal and other objects. Soon after the collection process was completed, he would begin to create different types of small book cases, whatnots, lamps and various original objects of art. Some of the whatnots had small lights added to them. They would also be ingeniously designed to represent many different forms, such as fish, flowers, books, statues and even animals. He was a master at using the manual jigsaw. Later, when he was able to purchase a small power saw, he developed great skill in cutting and shaping wood into likenesses of living things.

Sometime in December, when he had completed the task of constructing the many gifts to be distributed that year, he would either paint or stain the wooden pieces, finally placing a polished finish on the surfaces of those that were stained. The metal pieces were either left with natural surfaces, or he would polish them to a high luster.

Much work was required to bring the wooden surfaces to a satisfactory finish. He would first place a coat of stain, usually mahogany, on the surfaces. Then he would add the first coat of shellac. When the shellac was dry, the surfaces would be relatively smooth. He would then take very coarse sandpaper and roughen up the surfaces again. Following this, he would apply another coat of stain, followed by another coat of shellac and sanding once again—only this time he would use a finer grain of sandpaper. Depending upon the deepness of color he wanted the surfaces to be, he would repeat the process several times. When the proper tone was reached, no more stain was applied, but he would continue to apply shellac and repeat the sanding, now using an extremely fine grain of sandpaper. Demonstrating uncanny patience and a great desire for perfection, he would not stop until both the tone and finish that he wanted to see became a reality. The surfaces would become so shiny and slick that they would have the quality of mirrors. Unless he could satisfy himself that he had done a masterful job, he would not accept the product and therefore would not give it to anyone. When he had satisfied himself, however, the product was always a thing of beauty, and the recipient was always pleased and happy to receive it.

About one week before the college closed for the Christmas break, my father would deliver these beautiful gifts to certain selected faculty members and administrators. The selections were determined by whether he had received gifts from the recipients the previous year, or in the case of new people, whether he felt that they would respond to his giving. The most interesting part of his thinking about the gifts is that he always expected to receive cash or a check from those who had been so fortunate to receive one of his creations. For the most part, a return gift of money was the response. Now and then, he might receive a bag or crate of fruit or some gift that could be used in the household. This was by no means the preferred response. Although he would not get terribly upset if he got nothing but a Christmas card or a thank you note from someone to whom he had given a gift, it was a foregone conclusion that he would definitely not select such persons to receive gifts from him in the following year or future years.

Although some craftiness was present in the giving of Christmas gifts to people at the college, there was also a strong lesson being taught by my father to his children. Whether or not this is a good lesson is something that was questioned by several of his children. In one sense we learned a manifestation of the golden Rule, "Do unto others as you would have them do unto you." In another sense we learned a new rule, "Do everything you can for others and some of them will do for you."

The calculated risk of giving only to those who were likely to respond in the way that my father wanted them to respond, certainly goes beyond the Golden Rule. It also showed that he was capable of establishing an enterprising exchange at a festive time when most people are in a giving mood. He was not afraid to work hard at giving, but I believe he was working just as hard towards receiving. My father felt that receiving was no less important than giving.

As for me, I learned more about creative thinking from his gift-making activities than anything else. For him to envision the many wonderful objects in his mind before making them was to me the most impressive part of the whole process. I do not agree that receiving should be taken into consideration when the focus should be upon giving. What is important is his lesson on creativity.

THE IMPORTANCE OF COMPETITIVENESS

When parents or other adults play games with children, they sometimes will let the children win, even though the parent or other adult could have won. With my father, this was never the case. Whatever game he played, irrespective of the level of his competitor or competitors, he always played to win.

My father dearly loved to play checkers and cards. As I advanced from my early teenage years, I developed a rather formidable skill in playing checkers. Consequently, my father experienced great difficulty in beating me. Perhaps due credit should have been given to him for this development, since he was the one who taught me how to play the game in the first place. I did not, however, give him open credit, and as a result of that, he would become quite irritated with me for beating him so much.

When he would play cards with us children, he did everything he could to win. If he lost, he would become irritated. He was not malicious, but he did not want to stop playing until he was able to say that he had won a majority of the games. This was a lesson both in the dedication to winning and in perseverance. He never wanted to give up when trying to accomplish anything that he had started, nor did he want his children to give up. He would not lighten up just because he was playing against a child. Apparently, he felt that if the child was old enough and mature enough to learn a game, then the child should be able to handle the consequences of losing. It occurred to me later that my father was also saying to us that we could not be honest with ourselves unless we admitted that the purpose of playing games is to win. If we were to have pretended otherwise, we would have been trying to fool ourselves.

My own son has said to me many times that I was a fierce competitor when playing with him. Although I really never gave much thought to my being overly competitive against him, he probably is correct.

There is, however, more to the question of competition as it relates to living. Competitiveness is not just a matter of winning a game. It is a matter of teaching children that life itself may very well be a constant battle involving competition. To move forward in this world, one must be prepared to meet the competitive challenges.

Playing to win is not the only lesson derived from competition. My son and I spent a great deal of time shooting pool in our basement when he was quite young. Just as I developed greater skills at playing checkers than my father, my son developed greater skills at shooting pool than did I. He won most of the games. I recall rather vividly one day when I won the pool game fairly easily. This prompted him to say something that I considered to be insulting. I told him that he should never consider himself to be so good as a winner that he could belittle his opponent. I stated that he must apologize to me. He stood silently without apologizing. I then told him that he was not to use the pool table anymore until he apologized. Almost two years passed before he was allowed to shoot pool again. Having placed no time limit on the delivery of the apology, I decided to let him determine when to come to me with it. Although the apology eventually came and he was allowed to play again, the games were never the same.

The impact of the pool shooting incident was deeper with my son than I had expected. He felt so strongly that he had said nothing wrong that he was willing to give up the game rather than apologize. I am not sure even now that he accepts the fact that I was attempting desperately to teach him a lesson on politeness and humility, as well as the meaning of arrogance. Competitiveness should never be associated with the "I'm better than you syndrome." This, I think he learned, but I am not certain how effective the lesson was on humility and arrogance.

Competition can lead us to become our better selves. This was another lesson taught by my father. I was able to communicate this message to my son quite forcefully one day at the bowling alley. At that time, my son was nine years old. As we were bowling, we observed a child who was bowling on a lane next to us. The child was quite a good bowler, and from all indications, thought that he was perfect. However, each time he rolled the ball and did not get a strike, he would throw a temper tantrum, fall onto the floor and beat his clenched fists against the ball return mechanism. We observed his behavior. My son asked me if his own behavior was anything like the behavior of the other child. I explained to him that his behavior was not as bad as the other child, but there were similarities. At that moment, my son promised that he would change his behavior and said that he finally understood what I had been trying to point out to him about humility. Although I abhorred the way the other child was acting, his behavior presented me with a rare opportunity to further the very thing that my father taught about competing against one's self. The competitor within each of us challenging us to be better also deserves respect.

According to my father, competitiveness is part of life and is a part of the realities of human association. His actions made it clear that competitiveness should not interfere with compassion and understanding of the problems of others. Rather, he felt that if one were to maintain a competitive spirit, one would be better able to face bad times as easily as one faces good times. When the challenge appears to be a problem that cannot be resolved, that is the time to become the fierce competitor. If we succumb to the difficulties of the problem, the problem may overwhelm us. Competition is a means to solve the problem. Its value is found, not just in winning fun games, but also in winning the very games of survival.

LET HIM USE THE OLD BRUSHES

One of the most difficult things for me to understand about my father's teaching occurred when he first began to teach me how to paint houses. I wanted to know why I was required to use old, essentially worn-out brushes. I would say to him that I could learn a lot faster and a lot better if I had decent tools with which to work. This did not impress him, so I had to continue using the old and worn-out brushes for a long time.

I later realized there were two major reasons why I had to use the inferior tools. The first was that my father did not want me to mess up the good brushes, thereby leaving him with poor tools. The second, and by far the more important reason, was that old and worn-out brushes were adequate for a beginner. Once I progressed to a more advanced state, I would be a much better painter when I started using the good brushes. This theory was borne out with time, but it caused me an awful lot of hardship in learning how to paint. Admittedly, I became a highly skilled painter and was able to work as a painter even as a high school student. Long before paint rollers became popular, I could spread paint with a brush at a high rate of coverage and with great control.

During the summer of the year when I completed the ninth grade, I obtained a job with the Raleigh Housing Authority as a painter's helper. There were five painters, and each of them was assigned a helper. The main job of the helper was to prepare surfaces for painting. Window sills often had to be scraped or sanded to remove old paint. Cracks in walls had to be filled with spackling compound and furniture had to be moved about so that drop cloths could be placed on the floors.

The painting was done in occupied low-rent apartments provided by the city for economically depressed families. Only a few days passed before the painter for whom I was to serve as helper discovered that I could paint very well, probably as well as he could. His job immediately became easier, because I would help him, not just by moving things about the rooms that were being painted and preparing surfaces for readiness, but by sharing in the actual painting. Since each painter was responsible for a specified amount of work, he was able to reach his quota with far less effort than the other painters, simply because he did not have to do as much as they did. His work was supplemented by my efforts.

As the summer progressed, the apartment of the resident manager had to be painted. The foreman of the crew decided that he would, himself, take responsibility for painting this particular unit, because he wanted to make a special impression upon the

resident manager. Although he could have asked any
of the other painters to assist him in doing the manager's
apartment, he decided to ask me, the helper, to join him
for the job. He explained that he had observed how
carefully I had performed in painting for the person to
whom I was assigned. He concluded that I could do a
better job than all the painters who worked with him.
The foreman and I did all of the painting in the resident
manager's apartment. The next summer, and
thereafter, I was hired as a painter, with my own helper.

When I was a married college student, painting
houses formed the basic source of income for my
household. It helped pay the expenses of obtaining a
college education. When I was studying at the graduate
level, I was asked by a member of the staff in the
chemistry department if I could paint two rooms for him
without moving out or disturbing the furniture. I told
him that I could do it, but the job would take longer
than usual and that as a consequence, he would have
to pay a higher price than he would if the furniture were
moved about. He insisted that he did not want the
furniture moved and that he did not want the furniture
covered with drop cloths because he thought the drop
cloths might scratch the furniture. I painted the living
room and the dining room without the use of drop cloths
and did not move the furniture from its position in either
of the rooms. By being extremely careful, I did not get
any paint on the furniture and the staff member was
very pleased. Surely I would not have been prepared to
pull off such a hard task if I had not learned to paint
with the old and worn-out brushes—the way my father
taught me.

THE ART OF NEGOTIATING

As I was growing up my father would take me to work with him on Saturday. During those years the bursar of Meredith College was a man by the name of Mr. Hamrick. This man was known, as I learned later, to be a tough tightwad who guarded the finances of the college in "Midas" fashion.

One Saturday, I overheard a rather heated argument between my father and Mr. Hamrick over the hourly rate of pay my father was receiving. The rate that Mr. Hamrick was paying him at the time was twenty cents an hour. This amounted to a total of twelve dollars per week. The actual work hours were from seven in the morning to five in the afternoon, Monday through Friday and seven in the morning to noon on Saturday. Although only five hours were worked on

Saturday, he was paid for a full day, thus being credited for having worked a total of sixty hours each week. My father was trying to persuade Mr. Hamrick to raise the rate to twenty-five cents an hour so that his weekly salary would be increased by three dollars to a total of fifteen dollars. The basic argument from my father was that he was not making enough money to provide, even minimally, for his large family.

During the argument, my father gestured animatedly and raised his voice to a rather frightening level. I thought that his anger was going to lead to a physical fight. Despite this atmosphere, Mr. Hamrick did not appear to be impressed. Mr. Hamrick insisted that the college was not financially able to increase his or anyone else's salary at that time.

Although my father appeared to be in a heightened emotional state, he was not at all deterred by Mr. Hamrick's stubbornness or his obstinacy. He made it clear to Mr. Hamrick that Meredith College had already gotten from him far more work than the money he had been paid. He pointed out that he had been doing things that no janitor or handy man should be required to do, and he had done them willingly. He also let Mr. Hamrick know that no ordinary janitor or handy man could do all the things that he was doing anyway. Therefore the college was saving a lot of money at his expense. The time had now come for the college to make amends in some small way and pay him, not retroactively, but from that time forward at a more reasonable level. As he outlined to Mr. Hamrick the many family responsibilities he had and the unfair treatment by the college, Mr. Hamrick's argument began to soften. Somehow my father was able to cause him to see things his way. Finally, Mr. Hamrick gave in and told my father that beginning the next week, his salary would be fifteen dollars per week, or twenty-five cents per hour. Mr. Hamrick evoked from my father a pledge not to discuss what had transpired with anyone else—a pledge that my father readily honored.

The thing that stood out most to me in the argument with Mr. Hamrick was that my father never faltered in his goal. He let Mr. Hamrick say anything he wanted to say, but that did not change the circumstances around which the argument was taking place. He let Mr. Hamrick know in no uncertain terms that he had to have a salary adjustment and that the only acceptable conclusion that the discussion could reach would be an agreement between the two of them for an adjustment to be forthcoming. After hearing all the arguments, it was clear to me that my father was in complete charge of the discussion and that his point of view would prevail.

From this situation many years ago, I learned that if one is to negotiate a matter, be it a union contract or any other type of agreement, one is in the best position if he or she takes control of the deliberations. For me that message has served well. In my own dealings with union negotiators on the other side of the bargaining table, I have been highly successful in winning for the organization I represented the better side of any final agreement reached. The use of theatrics and persuasive arguments plays an equally important role in the negotiating process. When I think back to the time that I first observed my father and Mr. Hamrick holding a negotiation session, I become amused over the dramatic demonstration of acting ability shown by my father. He and Mr. Hamrick were the first business negotiators that I observed. They taught me that the successful negotiator is one who takes charge of the deliberations, puts on a show and lets the other side say anything that it wants to say.

Finally, the most powerful word that can be used in negotiations is "no." The negotiator should never be afraid to use this power word. All of this I learned from my father.

CHICKENS WERE DEAR TO MY FATHER'S HEART. IT APPEARS AS THOUGH HE KNEW EACH CHICKEN INDIVIDUALLY AND EACH OF THEM KNEW HIM.

DEALING WITH CHICKENS AND CATS

My family was very poor. As a consequence, many different schemes and innovative methods of acquiring food and money had to be developed, especially during those times when my father's wages were insufficient to carry the burden of providing the necessities for family maintenance.

As a direct result of this situation, my father decided at one time that he was going to raise chickens. The chickens would produce eggs to supplement the food source that seemingly was always less than the need required. He built a chicken coup in the backyard and bought two dozen baby chickens that the family called biddies. After a period of time, the biddies matured and became full grown chickens. Sure enough, the hens laid eggs, and the family was able to avail itself of this new food provision.

The eggs were helpful, but the time arose when one of the chickens was to be killed for cooking and consumption. An immediate family conflict developed because the children in the family had become attached to the chickens. Each of us tried to persuade my father to let all the chickens live. He insisted that one of the chickens had to be used for eating. So much care and love had been established for those chickens by my brothers and sisters that none of us could bring ourselves to the point where we could harm any of them, much less eat any part of one of them.

As things turned out, my father killed one of the chickens and enjoyed eating it. The rest of the family ate the gravy, but none of the meat of the chicken. This experience caused my father to change his mind about the endeared chickens and never again did he try to force upon us a meal that came from our own chickens. When the hens finally stopped laying eggs, he would give them to neighbors so they could eat them. The neighbors had no attachment that prevented them from enjoying the chickens and whoever was lucky enough to get one for free, was always happy to be on the receiving end.

Whereas chickens were special to the family, cats were an entirely different story. Everyone in my family was deathly afraid of cats. My father was the originator and perpetrator of this fear. On many occasions he would tell us of the time when he, as a child, participated in a community circus. One of the attractions of the circus was the great lion tamer. A cage was constructed in which the great lion tamer was to perform, and every cat that could be found was rounded up and placed in the cage. My father, dressed in a fancy uniform, entered the cage with a whip that he began cracking to make the cats respond to his commands. The response he got was a vicious attack from the cats as he cracked the whip. He was scratched unmercifully by them, and from that day until the day he died, he was dreadfully afraid of cats. His children continued this feeling towards cats. The fear remains, and none of us to this day can even stand to watch cats on television. When commercials come on for cat food or when cats are a part of any scene, we close our eyes.

When my oldest sister died, my other sisters and I went to California for her burial. Her son (my nephew) invited all of us to stay at his house while in California. As fate would have it, my nephew's wife was a cat lover and, as a consequence, owned several cats. Not knowing that there were cats in the house, my sisters, my wife and I, all of a sudden, found ourselves being inspected by four cats as we sat in the living room. Hysteria set in immediately. Except for my wife, everyone in the room either jumped on top of the sofa or chairs with absolutely no feet touching the floor. For several minutes, intelligent conversation was impossible.

Even worse than this behavior, was the way we treated our nephew's wife when she prepared dinner for us. We knew from the moment we saw the first cat that none of us could eat anything in that house. Eating in the presence of cats was an impossibility. My dear wife, knowing exactly what was going to happen, suggested to my nephew's wife that it was really not fair for her to take upon herself the task of preparing dinner for eleven people on a day when she had worked so hard already. We were going to take her family out to dinner. She was not too pleased at the beginning, but after a few minutes of encouragement, we convinced her that it was the proper thing to do. Although it was indeed the proper thing to do, she did not know that her cats were behind the whole thing.

My family's fear of cats can be seen in many different ways. For instance, if a member of the family is walking down the street and sees a cat on the same side of the street, that person will immediately cross the street to the other side. If the cat should cross the street also, the family member will turn around and go back the other way. If the family member happens to be driving a vehicle and a cat crosses the path of the vehicle, if it is at all possible, the family member will turn the vehicle around and go in the opposite direction. It doesn't matter that the route traveled is extended by the cat-crossing event. What is important is that the path followed by the cat is not crossed by the family member. This might ordinarily be considered a superstition, but my family labels it as unadulterated fear. When the family discussed superstitions, there was never even any mention of cats. The fear of cats is a part of my family culture.

SUPERSTITIONS

Although my father had a great fear of cats and taught his children also to fear cats, he had a rather humorous inclination toward superstitions. There are certain superstitions he regarded as just plain stupid, but he was afraid to scoff at them. He also made the children aware of any superstition with which he was familiar. Whenever the thirteenth of the month fell on a Friday, he would laugh at the possibility of being hit with bad luck if he happened to walk under a ladder on that day. Yet he would very carefully avoid walking under a ladder on Friday the thirteenth because he really was not sure whether the superstition might affect him. At the end of the day, he would boast of not having suffered any bad luck, but he was also quick to point out that he had not walked under a ladder either.

One of the funniest superstitions that he frequently

mentioned was the one suggesting that the finger would rot off if a person pointed it toward a graveyard. Since there was a cemetery within a city block from where we lived, there were many times that all of us had the opportunity to point toward a graveyard. If the finger was accidentally pointed toward the graveyard, the only way to prevent it from rotting off was to place the finger under the shoe and grind it into the dirt. I can recall many times that my brothers and sisters and I suffered the pain of grinding our fingers in the dirt under our shoes. This silly superstition, as my father put it, could be rough on the fingers of the forgetful.

Another superstition associated with the new year was that the first person to enter the house on New Year's Day must be male and not female, otherwise the house would be faced with bad luck for the entire year. If my mother or any of my sisters were in the house just before midnight on New Year's Eve, she and they would come out of the house. My father would enter and walk into each room before a female member of the family returned to the inside. Evidently this superstition also was an obsession in the home of my wife when she was a child, because she insists, even today, that I enter the house first and walk into each room after we have returned from a New Year's Eve party or some other event that might take us away from our home on that day. If we are at home when the new year comes in, just after midnight, she will walk outside the house with me. I will then enter the house ahead of her and walk throughout while she waits in one of the rooms where I have already walked.

The dinner menu at my house as a child on New Year's Day always included black-eyed peas cooked with hog's head. All the members of the family would stuff themselves with black-eyed peas. The reason was that the number of peas consumed by each person was somehow related to the number of dollars that person would acquire during the year. The more peas one ate, the more dollars one would receive during the year. Everyone always ate more black-eyed peas on New Year's Day than should have been eaten. An amusing, but not always comfortable aftermath of the pea-eating activity was the production of gas in our bodies. This led to a wind-breaking contest later in the day. Winners were determined by the loudest and longest expulsion of gas. Secondary winners were determined by the intensity of the odors. Every time someone would pass gas, the laughter would be almost uncontrollable.

One superstition, that was never explained to me, had to do with certain cards that might be dealt to my father while playing the game of Whist. If he received tens and fours, he felt that he had a bad hand. As a consequence, he would sulk and frequently claim that the opposition was cheating. If he did not get more than one ten or one four, this psychological effect was not experienced. Only if he got two or more of one or the other did he react. He could not make me understand why tens and fours created a problem, and until this day, I have not been able to develop a rationale for his disdain toward those denominations.

Other superstitions commonly feared in the Southland were treated sometimes with great respect by my family. Then, at times, some of them were scoffed at or completely ignored. Such things as putting a man's hat on a bed did not bother us at all, although that was supposed to be taboo. Opening an umbrella in the house was another one that did not bother most of the family, although some of the children felt queasy if they saw someone open an umbrella in the inside of the house. They were concerned and uneasy, thinking that if they did not adhere to the rule that umbrellas were not to be opened on the inside of a house, bad luck would come upon them.

Breaking mirrors was not greatly feared in the family. My father was able to convince the children that there was even some good in accidentally breaking a mirror. He decided that seven years of bad luck meant at least seven more years of life. If one were faced with this unfortunate consequence of breaking a mirror, there was an inherent period of security associated with it. On the other hand, my father did not advocate breaking mirrors as a means of extending one's life, whether with or without the bad luck.

THE FAMILY LANGUAGE

The use of profanity by any member of my family in the presence of another member of the family was strictly prohibited. My father and mother considered it to be an unforgivable sin for one of their children to use a foul word of any kind. There were some words that really are not classified as foul, but we could not use them because my parents felt that they sounded bad. There were words that should have been acceptable, but members of the family were forced to coin certain code words or phrases to describe situations that could not be discussed in ordinary terms. Some of the words and/or phrases for which substitutes were used are as follows:

BREASTS - There is no way that either the word "breast" or "breasts" could have been used by anyone in my family in regular conversation. Several different words were used to refer to breasts. The word used most was "ninnies." Even when someone mentioned the word "ninnies," there was always a look of anxiety on the face, because the user of the word was never certain whether there would be some scolding for having directed another's mind to the breast area. A single breast was, of course, referred to as a "ninny." Another term used for the breast was "ninny pie." Although I am not certain as to the derivation of this term, I suspect that it came from the concept of breast-feeding, whereby a baby would feed on a "ninny pie" instead of the breast, as others would say. Although I do not know what a "purnie ball" is, my family referred to women who were well endowed as having "purnie balls" rather than large chests. The children in the family got many a laugh from being able to point out a person with "purnie balls." The boys, in particular, liked to talk about "purnie balls." To use the word "teat" or "nipple" in connection with the breast, or to use the word "tit" was as bad as having used the Lord's name in vain. The only place these words could be heard would be some place other than in our home.

SEX ORGANS - Anatomically, the words "vagina" and "penis" carry no negative connotation whatsoever. Nonetheless, in the family, one would not dare use one of these words. For the female sex organ, two different words were used, "tudy" and "plop." There is no way of knowing whether one took preference over the other or whether there was a variance in meaning. The more commonly used of the two was "tudy," but even here, the word was used with great reluctance. For the male sex organ, the name assigned was that of "tee-pot." If the name had been "teapot," it might be easy to understand the association, the teapot having a spout through which either hot water, tea or coffee is poured. In this case, "tee-pot" represents the word for penis. Apparently, it was being compared with the spout on a teapot.

THE BUTTOCKS - Occasionally a child might have gotten away with saying the word "rump" in reference to the buttocks, although that was not often. If the child felt strong enough to put our parents to a test, the word "butt" might be used. This was not often either. The word coined by my mother for the buttocks was "bushum." If one talked about "bushum," one was clearly talking about the buttocks. Modifiers were frequently used with "bushum," such as flat, big, fat, slack and huge. The big "bushum" was always the one that caused the kids to snicker. My mother seemed to take delight in pointing out a big "bushum" because she knew that it would cause a good laugh. Such terms as rectum and even posterior, were too strong to be used freely.

BATHROOM - There was only one good reason why the word "bathroom" was not used by the members of my family. The reason was simply that for most of the years when children were being raised, there was no bathroom in the house. The place of relief could have been appropriately called the "toilet," "lavatory," or "rest room," but that was not the case. The actual name used for the lavatory was "The Jakes." If one had to use the lavatory, the statement would be made that, "I have to go to The Jakes." The likely origin of the term is that of a man who lived in the neighborhood by the name of

Jake who was not held in high esteem by the family. Going to "The Jakes" was like a dog using a fireplug, except in this situation, the fireplug was a man named "Jake." In reality, the bathroom was whatever bedroom in which the big tin tub was placed when one took a bath.

BOWEL MOVEMENT - If one had to go to the lavatory to have a bowel movement in our house, that person had to "go to 'The Jakes' to grunt." The word "feces" was never used by my family as far as I can remember, to say nothing of more vulgar words commonly used for excrement. The sound that is sometimes made while one is having a bowel movement is what gave rise to the term "grunt."

SANITARY NAPKINS - If one of my sisters needed a sanitary napkin, she would say she needed a "samich." Even the trade name of Kotex was not allowed to be used by the girls in the family. As far as I know, the only brand of sanitary napkin used during the childhood years of my sisters was Kotex, but never was the Kotex box referred to by that name. Then, the box was always called a box of "samiches."

MENSTRUATION - The name used for menstruation was "eeding." This word was apparently coined from "bleeding," simply by dropping the "bl." During the menstrual period, no sister would have the nerve to say that she was bleeding, so the supposedly less offensive term, "eeding," was used.

PREGNANCY - If a woman was pregnant, no one in my family would use that word to describe the situation.

Anyone who was pregnant, was "Annie." The origin of this connotation is not known. If the pregnant person just happened to have been named Annie, this would give rise to many good laughs, because time and time again, someone would say that "Annie is Annie." Of course, if an unmarried girl or woman was "Annie," she was looked upon as having committed a great wrong.

DRUNK - When an individual was observed in a drunken state from having consumed too much alcohol, the individual was said to "have on shoes." The word "drunk" was not allowed to be used by the children in the family. How the term is related to the wearing of shoes, or if there is a relationship, is something that has never been made clear. But everyone knew exactly what was being said if one was described as "having on shoes." The individual "having on shoes" was drunk. Some people in the neighborhood were watched very closely by the children, because they tended to "have on shoes" more than others. The children always got a big charge out of being able to report that someone was in the neighborhood who "had on shoes."

TREATS OR GOODIES - When someone in the family was going to offer some special treat, such as buying ice cream or a fancy dessert for everyone, that person would be "opening up a keg of nails." To hear the expression, "I'm going to open up a keg of nails," was something that all family members welcomed. The comparison between opening a keg of nails and giving a special treat to the family is perhaps equivalent to having the necessary equipment—nails, to do something constructive. If the keg is unopened, the nails are there, but are not necessarily available for use. Only when

the keg is opened and the nails can be accessed is the
situation favorable. Thus, opening a keg of nails (giving
a special treat) was something that pleased everyone
because they knew that they were going to have access
to something good.

HOMELINESS OR UGLINESS - If a child in the
family were to call another person ugly, and either of
my parents found out, that child stood the risk of being
punished. On the other hand, if the children were to
say that another person was "toby struck," there was
no risk. Someone in the family coined the term "toby
struck" to mean homeliness or ugliness. As far as can
be determined, the term originated from the slang word
"toby," which means cigar. If one strikes, or pounds a
cigar against a solid surface, such as a table top, the
cigar is crushed into a pile of brown mess. If an
individual brings to mind the results of a cigar struck
against a solid surface, that individual is certainly not
very attractive. In fact, that individual is "toby struck."
To laugh at someone who had been called "ugly" would
more than likely lead to a spanking by one or the other
of my parents.

CUTTING A DECK OF CARDS - My father always
wanted others to think that he could control the
distribution of playing cards by cutting the deck in a
certain manner. He would have one believe that he
could determine to whom the aces were dealt, as well
as all the other high cards. He supposedly had voodoo-
like powers over the cards if he was allowed to touch
them by cutting the deck before the deal took place. He
coined a word to describe his actions. If he should say
that he was putting his "theatical" on the cards,

everyone was supposed to know that he had determined who was going to get what. Even though all the players knew that his "theatical" had no real effect upon the distribution of the cards, he would claim to have known what each player was holding before the cards were played. Out of fatherly respect, no one, as far as I know, ever pointed out the fantasy of his "theatical." There were times, however, when he would voluntarily admit that the "theatical" did not work. In such cases, he would have come out as the loser.

NICKNAMES - All ten of the Nichols children had some kind of nickname. In some cases, there was more than one name. In other cases, there was only one. The origins of the nicknames were not always clear, but in some cases they were obvious. The ten nicknames are:

> **Bae:** The youngest of the children was named Cynthia. She was called "Bae" as a derivative of baby. Even today, she is still referred to as "Bae" or "the baby," even though she has a husband and a grown son.
> **Dot:** The nickname "Dot" is a short version of Doris.
> **Mot:** Margaret has always been known as "Mot."
> **Unks:** For many years, "Unks" was the name used for Owen. A brother-in-law was the first to start using the nickname. He contended that Owen acted like an old man when he was a child and therefore should be called something that suggested age. He derived "Unks" from the term, "Uncle."
> **Sis:** Pearl was and is known as "Sis." She probably was more sisterly in her behavior than

the other girls; that is, she was the epitome of femininity and softness. For some reason, "Sis" seemed like the only name appropriate.

Beh and Ree Ree: Marie's nickname was usually "Beh." This came from her middle name, which was Elizabeth. She was called "Ree Ree" in her latter years, this coming from the vowel sound at the end of her first name.

Skonimo: The strangest nickname given to any of the Nichols children was that of "Skonimo," the name given to brother Edward. From what this name was derived remains a mystery even today. For some unknown reason, members of the family would say when questioned, "He just looked and acted like Skonimo."

Gene, Short Stuff and Lefty: Eugene was always known to the family as "Gene." Occasionally, he would be referred to as "Short Stuff" by persons outside the family. This name emanated from his rather short stature. He was the shortest of the four male children. Strangely enough, he never considered the nickname, "Short Stuff," to be offensive. Being the only natural left-handed member of the family, some people would call him "Lefty." This name was used frequently when he played softball, since he was an excellent left-handed pitcher.

Sate: Although she was called Sarah Leigh— her given name—most of the time, when a shorter name was used, it was "Sate"

Willie and Blo: The first-born of the children was William Henry, Junior. During his early years, he was called "Willie." As the years passed, he used to say that he sometimes behaved like El Diablo, whom he considered to be the "devil." As a consequence of that, he was called "Blo" for the rest of his life. "Blo," of course, was short for El Diablo.

THIS IS "THE CABIN," BUILT FROM SCRATCH BY MY FATHER, WITH THE HELP OF HIS CHILDREN. IT WAS A PLACE ENJOYED BY FAMILY, NEIGHBORS AND FRIENDS FOR MANY, MANY YEARS. IN REALITY, IT SERVED AS A COMMUNITY CENTER.

THE MAKING OF WINE

Curiosity about something my father did once a year caused me to learn how to make wine. For many years he would gather together various products to make a home-brew. I really did not understand what he was using for the creation of the final product, but I was so impressed with the manner with which he went about mixing the components and carefully placing them in special vats and attentively monitoring the progress for several weeks at a time, I decided that it was a challenging process worthy of learning. I asked him if he would teach me how to make the home-brew, but he declined, saying that children had no business making beer. I must have been about nine years old at the time and really felt that he was turning water into wine. I was determined to find out how it was done. Since he would not teach me how to make the home-brew, I decided I would develop a process of my own to make wine.

The very next summer, I spent hour after hour gathering plums from trees that I had located, primarily on the campus of Meredith College, as well as trees near the cemetery, near the house and other places close by. I was able to pick about half a bushel of plums. I also acquired several one-gallon glass bottles from the kitchen at the college. These were bottles in which mayonnaise and pickles had been packaged. I bought one three-cent yeast cake for each of the bottles to accelerate fermentation, and my mother gave me some sugar to use, after I explained what I was going to do. It took me several weeks to complete the process. I did not think that my father was paying any attention to what I was doing, but when I finished the job and bottled the wine, he took it away from me and lectured to me on the subject of children using alcohol. He said that I was too young to drink wine and had no business keeping the bottles of wine I had produced. He did, however, commend me for making such a fine batch of wine. He and his friends consumed every bottle and as far as I know enjoyed every drop. For me, that was the first and last wine I ever made, but I satisfied myself that it could be done, by me.

THE VALUE OF VERSATILITY

If my father needed to do something with his hands and had not had the experience of having done it before, he would either learn from someone else how to do whatever he needed to do or he would teach himself how to do it. I cannot remember anything that he ever wanted to do manually that he did not do. He could do more different things than anyone else I ever knew. In the case of mental functions, he always demonstrated a superior ability to figure out how things worked and how to solve problems. There was nothing that he could not do if he chose to do it. Unfortunately, he did not have the privilege or the benefit of acquiring the educational background that would have placed him in a position to achieve momentous financial gain.

If he had been trained at a higher academic level, there is no telling what he might have accomplished in life or to what heights he might have risen. In actuality, he was a philosopher, carpenter, plumber, painter, bricklayer, cement finisher, wood craftsman, electrician, mechanic and, above all, a teacher. To his credit is the fact that he taught me all the skills that he possessed.

When I graduated from high school and was voted by my classmates as "the Most Versatile" member of the class, I began even then to understand and appreciate more of the things my father had taught me, not the least of which was to develop a method of problem solving that would equip me with the necessary tools to cope with whatever might confront me. His teaching was also in great evidence when I was voted as "The Most Scholarly" member of my high school graduating class. Having been encouraged by my ability to do many things successfully, I began to devote some time and attention to what career objectives I should seek. I decided that I wanted to be a mathematician and a fashion designer of women's clothes.

Armed with the strong interest in becoming a mathematician, I took advantage of a scholarship presented to me by Shaw University in Raleigh and registered as a math major. On the same day that I registered, I went back to my high school to see some of my teachers and to let them know that I was now a bona fide college student. When I saw my former history teacher, she asked me how her husband and I had gotten along. I told her that I had not seen her husband. She suggested that I go back to the campus and see him. Her husband was the chairman of the chemistry department at Shaw and thought that I was coming to Shaw as a chemistry major.

Later, as I entered the chairman's office, he asked me where I had been all day. I told him that I had gone through the registration process and then went back to my high school to see some of my former teachers, including his wife. He asked me how I could register without coming to see him. To this I replied that I did not know it was necessary for me to come to him. I had completed the registration without any difficulty. He then asked me what was my major, and I told him that I was a math major. This surprised him because he had been led by his wife to believe that I would be majoring in chemistry. In that connection, he had arranged a job for me as a laboratory assistant in the chemistry department. This was an unusual arrangement, because new freshman students had not been offered such positions in the past. I was receiving the offer strictly on the basis of my high school record and upon the recommendation of the chairman's wife, who knew that I needed a job.

When the chairman told me that I could not have the job unless I majored in chemistry, I asked him if he would have any objections if I went back through the system and changed my major. He said that it would be fine with him if I did. As a consequence, I went back and changed my major from math to chemistry on the first day I entered college, not because I had lost interest in math, but because the job was more important to me at the time than the major. I went on to earn a degree in chemistry and continued to earn an advanced degree in chemistry as well.

The importance of versatility, stressed by my father, became more apparent to me as I experienced various reactions and admonitions from those who were my supervisors on several jobs I held. I still get a chuckle out of some of the things said to me. My first recollection goes back to the time when I was about to leave the

United States Army. My term as a commissioned officer was over, and I was in Korea. When I told the officer in command of my outfit that I was going to leave active duty, he said to me, "You are making a terrible mistake by not staying in the Army because you are a natural leader, and you have a great military career ahead of you." I did not listen and left the Army. I had been convinced by my father that there was no one thing I could do better than any other thing.

My brief Army career was followed by additional educational training, and ultimately a position as an associate professor of chemistry at a college in South Carolina. After a little more than two years in this job, I decided to accept a job as a research chemist with the United States Naval Research Laboratory in Washington, DC. When I informed the dean at the college that I was leaving, he said, "You are making a mistake by getting out of the teaching profession because you are a natural teacher and will be depriving yourself and your students of a great talent." Again, I did not listen and reported to the Naval Research Lab. This job lasted for about three years, until I was offered another government position as a technical analyst with a different agency. Just as before, my immediate supervisor said to me, "You should not leave this job, because you are a natural researcher and you are giving up a wonderful opportunity to make a serious contribution to science." Again, I left and became a technical analyst, later becoming head of my division.

Time again brought me to another job offer as an administrator at a major university in Washington, DC. Already having been told that I had blown three careers, I decided to accept the position in higher education, but not without being told by the head of the government agency for which I was working that I again was making a terrible mistake. He said that I was in a position to move to the top of the ladder and the best thing I could do for my family and myself was to stay with the federal government.

What I learned most from these admonitions is that my father had influenced me to do the best job I could in whatever situation I found myself. One should never be deluded into thinking that any given achievement is the ultimate achievement. The truly versatile person is never satisfied, for there is always something else that can and should be done. There is always one more bridge that has not been crossed or one more road that has not been mapped or traveled. In a rather simplistic way, my father gave me the answer to the question raised by Voltaire in 1759 when he asked, "If this is the best of [all] possible worlds, what then are the others?" My father's answer, without hesitation or reservation, was that the question includes a faulty conjecture. It is incorrect to conclude that this is the best of all possible worlds, when the best of all possible worlds is yet to come. The other worlds remain to be discovered.

WHO IS IN CHARGE?

All too often there were questions raised in the minds of my sisters and brothers, as well as in my own mind, concerning parental authority. As I grew up watching my mother and father, I developed such questions where parents were involved such as, was the mother in charge of the children, or was the father in charge? Was there shared authority between the mother and the father, or was there some competitive thing going on between the two parents to determine who was in charge?

There was a tendency on the part of the children to take advantage of the parents, especially when it appeared that permission to buy something or to do something desired by the children required the agreement of only one parent. When agreement was received from one parent, the children would carefully avoid mentioning the matter to the other parent. This was done so that the agreement could not be voided by the other side.

At times, the children would also play one parent against the other. If it was clear that both parents had to approve the acquisition of some desired item or request, the parent most likely to agree was always approached first. After agreement was obtained from this parent, the other parent would not be asked to approve the acquisition or request, but to give support to the decision already made by the first parent. This was done to make the parents feel that there was no conflict between them.

The "who is in charge" question goes far beyond the parent/child relationship. It is a question that enters almost every phase or element of society. It is also a question that either reveals or reflects the hunger for power that so many human beings demonstrate. Those who station themselves in position to order or dictate to others that which is to be done are saying, in effect, "We are in charge!"

On the other hand, those who are in need may very well be looking for someone who is in charge in order to get an active response to satisfy their needs. The response could come either from whoever is in charge, or by a directive from whoever is in charge. This represents a search for a different kind of power—a search not for the egotistical pleasure of the holder or bearer of that power, but for the benefit of the recipient with whom that power is used.

There are also instances where power is used to hurt someone rather than to help. This means that those in charge have more than one option for use of the power that goes with being in charge. For example, if a military commander is responsible for the protection of some territory, he or she might decide to destroy an identifiable enemy rather than risking the possibility of an attack by the enemy. Thus, the power of the protector may have been used to destroy an enemy that really was not a threat. Power is not always used properly.

Closer to everyday living is the example of a police officer who is in charge of protecting ordinary citizens or an ordinary community. Although the uniform worn by the officer or the marked car driven may be symbols of power, the most powerful means of carrying out the officer's responsibilities is the weapon worn. The weapon may be visible, or it may be concealed. In either case, it is the true representation of authority and power. Of major concern is the way an armed police officer views the circumstances under which the weapon should be used. Almost always, the weapon is used for self protection of the officer and not for the protection of someone else. Worse still is that police brutality can come about because of the power of the gun. Without the gun, police officers would be less prone to brutalize. The gun reduces the fear of retaliation. As a consequence, the "who is in charge" question can easily be answered by a police officer by saying, "My gun and I are in charge"

There are times when the effectiveness of government is affected by the "who is in charge" question. The question arises at local, state and national levels of government. Where there is confusion over who is responsible for accomplishing various tasks, the tasks usually are not completed in the most efficacious way. Also, there can be so many different functions involved in government that it is difficult to determine who is in charge at all times. At the national level, the President of the United States is supposedly in charge, but the extent to which the President can control all aspects of government is minuscule at best. If government is looked upon in a pyramidal manner, the President certainly sits at the point on top, but to have a controlling effect at the base is virtually impossible. The same can be said about governors, mayors, county executives and others.

Who is in charge of the church? Is God in charge? How nice it would be to answer definitively that God really is in charge of the church and that popes, bishops, preachers, Christian educators, lay leaders, lay members and everybody else associated with the church are simply following God's orders. Unfortunately, such an answer is not applicable to the behavior of many. Words and deeds are not always compatible. Whereas many Christians and even some non-Christians would suggest that God is in charge of the church, their actions would lead the world to believe that they, and they alone, are in charge of the church. However, if they were to think seriously about a particular verse of the Holy Bible (Matthew 16:18) when Jesus said, "Upon this rock I will build my church; and the gates of hell shall not prevail against it," they would understand clearly that the church belongs to God. Jesus did not say that He would build somebody else's church upon the rock, but that He would build His own church there. If the church was built by God, through His Son, Jesus, then God must be in charge of the church. Since that is the case, there is no "who is in charge" question that should apply to the church.

When it comes down to "who is in charge" within the family, certainly the parents bear a strong responsibility. If parents do not guide their children and teach them authoritatively the developmental aspects of life, then parents have not done what they are supposed to do. If children do not respect the authority of parents, then children have not done what they are supposed to do. In reality, every member of the family is in charge of something. When that something is identified, defined and carried out, there will no longer be a question about who is in charge of family life.

WHEN DOES CHILD-REARING STOP?

Unlike most parents of today, and even during the years I was growing up, my father had definite thoughts and rules regarding when parents should shift from the child-rearing state to letting the child be self-sufficient. His feelings on this matter caused him more conflict with his children than any other matter I can identify. He felt that parents should stop serving as guardians for their children when the children finished high school. He also felt that after high school, children must go to work and share their earnings with their parents.

My father's position first became clear to me when my oldest sister finished high school and got a job doing domestic work. The first time she received her money for working, my father asked her for a definite amount to be used for food and other household expenses. She balked at the notion of giving part of the money to my father. This led to a serious confrontation between them. My father made it clear to my sister that she would now have to contribute to the financial needs of the family just as he did. She resisted and solicited the help of my mother in trying to get my father to change his mind and let her keep all the money. The amount, by the way, was only a few dollars. She was not successful in her endeavor, and therefore she shared her earnings with the family. This represented the establishment of a new rule for all the children who reached the stage when they were no longer in school, continued to stay at home and earned money. None of the children fully accepted the rule, but all were forced to adhere to it.

The oldest of the children was a brother who left home as a teenager to live with my mother's uncle in Washington, DC. Whether this brother left home because of the rule of sharing his earnings, I never knew. It was years before he came back to Raleigh to visit the family. The younger children, myself included, did not even see this brother until we had become teenagers. My suspicion is that he fled the household in Raleigh to avoid the rule set forth by my father. After serving several years in the military, this brother returned home for a visit and decided to stay. Although he lived at home after his return, he was not subjected to the rule that required him to share his earnings.

Another brother also escaped the rule because he won a scholarship to college, thus making him the first of the children to enroll in a college. His college education was interrupted by World War II, and he never graduated. The significance of his escape from the rule is manifested in the allowance my father made for his continuing education. Even though he graduated from high school, this brother was not required to adhere to the rule. My father had sufficient interest in his children's education to waive the rule for any who extended his/her education beyond the high school level. In spite of his meager formal education, my father still appreciated the value of education for his children.

Another brother left home to join the Civilian Conservation Corps (CCC) when he was eighteen years old. This brother had more difficulty with my father than any of the other children. The two of them seemed unable to get along with each other. There were many times when this brother and my father would come to blows. When they did fight, my brother would usually take off, running away from my father, who would chase him until he just could not run any more. To my knowledge my father never caught up with him. After staying away from home a few hours, this brother would return. Neither he nor my father would pursue the matter further. There was never any lingering animosity associated with any given incident. Time seemed always to erase the problem of the moment, but unfortunately, new problems were certain to develop. Over time, my father gradually relented and allowed the children to contribute their earnings if they wished, but he did not require them to do so.

Is there a time when parents can say that the child-rearing days are over? My father would have answered with a resounding, "Yes." He would have said that parents who take their children through high school have done as much as they should be required to do in rearing them. What the children learn and do after that, they should learn and do on their own. Further, my father would have said that children have an obligation to their parents to return something after

the parents have given so many years of care and
maintenance to the children. My father would also have
said that children inevitably reach a point where there
is a transition from childhood to adulthood, and that is
the point where parental responsibilities change. The
basic change to which he would have been referring is
the diminution, if not the cessation, of parental
responsibility.

My father's views on the transition from childhood
to adulthood are probably not consistent with the views
of most parents of today. They may not have been
consistent with the views of most of his contemporaries
either, but they raise the interesting question as to when
and if parents are ever relieved of the responsibility of
child-rearing.

There are many instances where children reach an
age when they should be qualified for adulthood, but
continue to behave like children. In such cases, parents
tend to feel obligated to offer the same kind of care and
attention that they did when the children were young
enough to be considered as, and called, children. Thus,
for some parents, child-rearing never stops.

Another group of parents for whom child-rearing
seems never to stop, is that group of parents who want
and attempt to exercise control over the lives of their
children for as long as they can.

These two patterns bear absolutely no relationship
to the position taken by my father. He showed no
interest in wanting to control the lives of his children
for any period of time. He just wanted his children to
understand that they, too, must take upon themselves
part of the responsibility of their upbringing at a certain
stage in their lives. Parents are sometimes encouraged

to continue to treat their sons and daughters as children into adulthood by the children themselves. Some children do not want to lose the comfort of parental care.

My father's teachings led me to analyze the subject of child-rearing as it relates to child-giving and child-caring and to ponder the interrelationships.

On the basis of his example and discussions, I would distinguish among the three as follows:

CHILD-REARING - In the process of rearing a child, parents are expected to offer sound and usable guidance that will assist the child in developing into a responsible adult. Associated with child-rearing is the parental responsibility for providing material necessities and health care. A closely connected, yet major role of parents, is to provide (create and maintain) a secure environment in which children may learn and grow.

CHILD-CARING - Child-rearing and child caring are inexplicably intertwined. If children have been reared properly, parents will have inherently provided a measure of child care. That care may have required sacrifice by the parents, but it is a necessary component. A major element of child care is to bring love to that child. The parent's responsibility is to help the child develop emotionally, socially and spiritually. The parent will instill in the child personal and social values—the key is to make sure these values will serve the child well as he/she interacts with others in whatever situations occur.

CHILD-GIVING - Assuming that children have been given the fundamental requirements for reasonable development to maturity from a physical standpoint and that the intangibles, such as love, concern and compassion, have been freely offered, the parent must decide how much more children should be given as they attain maturity. Many parents are able to provide special experiences such as piano lessons, travel, sports opportunities, trips to the zoo, college education, a personal computer and so on. Other parents may have to be more creative to offer some of these special experiences without the costs normally associated therewith. Child-giving can be a very positive aspect in the parent-child relationship. However, it can also be the primary method used by parents who want to exercise control over their children's lives. One of the easiest ways to misguide children is to shower them with too much material giving. There are many confused adults in the world whose confusion came from receiving more from their parents than could be justified. As strange as it may sound, there may be some useful benefits available to families in poorer circumstances, since it is unlikely that the children of these families can be given too much. My father gave us all that he could materially, but it was not as much as I am able to give my children. The best part of what he gave us was his wisdom, his encouragement, his love and the teachings that have remained with us as we accepted the responsibilities of adults and eventually parents of our own children. I may have been remiss in giving my own children far more than my father could have ever given me. If I had followed his teachings, I would have limited what I provided for the children of my own household. However, I do not believe that my giving has had a negative effect upon their development, and I am following his example in sharing what I have with my children.

FOOLING THE FISH

My father probably gave fish more credit for being smart than most other people. I am absolutely certain that he felt that fish had minds of their own. He insisted that the brain of a fish was more highly developed than humans realized. As a consequence, he took it upon himself to outsmart the very fish he was attempting to catch, wherever and whenever. To him this was the art of fishing.

My father would devise all kinds of schemes to outsmart the fish. When his catch was large, he felt triumphant and victorious because he had been successful in fooling the fish and luring them into his trap. One of his favorite means of fishing was to find a spot along the river bank where a trotline could be placed and left undetected by other fishermen for a few days. The trotline, as he constructed it, consisted of a heavy rope-like line that could withstand about two hundred pounds of stress and stretch without breaking. Usually the length would be about fifty yards. Several rather large fishhooks were tied to the line, each baited with various types of worms and meat. In some cases, artificial lures would also be attached to the line. At one end of the line, a lead ball, weighing about three pounds, would be attached. The purpose of this was to keep the line submerged below the surface of the river, thus, serving as an anchor. The other end of the line would be tied to a heavy rock or to the trunk of a tree. Once the line had been fully prepared and tied down, my father would throw the lead ball as far out into the river as he could. He would not throw the line straight across, but at an angle, so that he could take advantage of its full length. The river was not wide enough for the line to be thrown straight across. If he did not throw it far enough at first, he would pull it in and throw it out again, checking each time to see whether he had lost any of the hooks or bait in the process.

When he was satisfied that the trotline was properly positioned, he would then try to camouflage the end that was tied down by covering it with branches from trees and bushes and with weeds and tree leaves. With everything in place, he would leave the trotline in the river and come back to check it every three or four days. If the ideal situation existed, there would be a fish on each hook. Seldom was that the case, however, but seldom also was the line devoid of fish. There were times when he had caught fifteen to twenty pounds of fish on that one trotline. If the catch did not meet his expectations, quite often he would remark that the fish had outsmarted him and eaten up his bait. Also, when the catch was low, he would move the trotline to another location.

The first real lesson I ever got in fishing was "how to bait the hook." My father would let me use one of his bamboo poles, equipped with a rather short line as well as a cork and hook. I really wasn't too happy about putting the slimy, wiggly worms on the hook, but after seeing how easy it was, and certainly after catching my first fish, I didn't mind it at all. The thing I hated more than baiting the hook was having to take off the fish when caught. I was afraid that the fish would cut me with its fins. This was not an unfounded fear, since I had seen my father get his fingers cut by fish fins on several occasions.

Once I became proficient in using my father's pole and line, he took his equipment away from me and made me get my own. With my interest now at a very high level, I had no problem with acquiring my own gear, although I did experience some difficulty in finding suitable bamboo poles.

Although other forms of fishing gear were available, my father never abandoned the use of bamboo poles in his fishing. Even when he upgraded his equipment to include a rod and reel, the most reliable piece he would depend upon was the old bamboo pole. His use of the rod and reel required some learning on his own. Even now, I can picture him standing in the middle of the street in front of our house day in and day out tossing the line from the reel and slowly winding it back in as if he had caught a fish. He would go through this exercise for several hours at a time, and he kept it up for weeks. He must have had the rod and reel for as long as three months before he built up sufficient courage to head for the water and use them in a real situation. The practice period was not always easy, for on many a day he threw the line in such a way that it got tangled in the tree limbs hovering above the street surface. Each time he got the line tangled, he would become quite irritated and could be heard fussing to himself. The time did come, however, when he considered himself to be an expert with the rod and reel. This feeling gave him even more confidence in being able to fool the fish, because it added significantly to his fishing versatility.

One form of fishing with which my father was not familiar was that of gigging. I brought this type of fishing to his attention. When I was still in elementary school, I worked as a bicycle-riding delivery boy at a grocery store. The butcher for whom I worked asked me if I could go gigging with him one night, mainly to carry equipment and hold the light for him. Having not the slightest notion how gigging was done, I accepted the invitation out of curiosity and, of course, contingent upon my parent's approval. My mother was somewhat reluctant about my going with the man because she thought that fishing at night would be unsafe under any circumstances for a youngster like myself. My father, on the other hand, had no reservations whatsoever about my going. He thought it would be a fine, exciting experience for me, and he knew that I would come back and describe for him every detail of the process. Although with a fair degree of hesitation and disturbing uncertainty, my mother finally agreed to let me go.

I learned that gigging was a form of spear fishing. The thing that caught my interest at the very beginning was the pair of hip boots that the butcher had brought along for me to wear. I had no idea there was anything that could be worn to keep one from getting wet while walking in water that was more than three feet deep.

Yet, these rubber boots that covered from the lower part
of the body almost to the waist, did just that. While
walking through the water, I kept thinking to myself
that both the butcher and I were defying nature. When
I realized that we could see fish swimming in the murky
water just by shining a bright light on the surface of
the water, I was taken aback even more. The gigging
device used by the butcher to spear the fish seemed quite
simple, but it was very effective. Every time a fish was
caught, the butcher appeared to have entered a state of
ecstasy. I do believe that he, like my father, was feeling
as though he had fooled the fish. We must have walked
about a mile down the creek without coming out of the
water. When we did come out, I was carrying a bag
stuffed with fish.

Upon arriving back home, although it was rather
late at night, I explained to my father very carefully
exactly what had transpired, as well as what he would
need to be able to fish by gigging. He was excited about
the possibilities. Not too many days thereafter, he
equipped himself with the necessary gear and headed
for the creek to try to fool the fish by gigging them. He
had now increased his fishing capabilities with a
satisfying new method.

Still another method used by my father in his
attempts to fool the fish was something he called "cage-
fishing." It was never clear to me whether or not one
could purchase the necessary cage for this type of
fishing, but to my father it did not matter anyway. He
gathered his own materials and put together the
equipment he needed for cage-fishing.

He would start by cutting several pieces of wood,
two inches wide and two inches thick into lengths of
three feet. He would then cut little pieces of metal from

tin cans and form them into L-shaped brackets. Handling the tin was tedious because of the sharp edges, and he had to be exceedingly cautious to avoid cutting himself. Once he had enough of the brackets, he would use them to hold the wood together in forming a cube-shaped frame, three feet-by-three feet on each side. Except for one side, the cube would then be covered with chicken wire. On the open side of the cube, he would attach chicken wire in which he had constructed a swinging door, one foot square. The door was framed with thin pieces of wood, with little spring-like devices that caused it to close on its own when pushed open and released. The door could be opened toward the inside of the cage, but not toward the outside. Hanging from the top of the cage and suspended at the center was another small cubic device that was to hold the bait. This device was also made from chicken wire. The basic idea behind cage-fishing was to have the fish swim into the cage through the trap door to get to the bait, without being able to consume it. Once in the cage, the trap door prevented escape.

When the cage was ready for placement in the water, he would take it to the river and submerge it at a point close to the bank and tie it to a rock, tree trunk or some other suitable holding structure. Just as he had tried to camouflage the exposed part of the trotline, he also tried to hide the lead wire that held the cage in place. Once properly situated, he would leave the cage in the water and come back every two or three days to check it and remove any fish trapped therein. This was a highly successful operation, because he would always find fish in the cage. He took great delight and pride over the fact that he had found still another way to fool the fish.

KNOW WHEN TO QUIT

Spending too much time on any one activity tends to deny an individual the joys and privileges associated with variety. If anyone ever believed, with heart and soul, that "variety is the spice of life," it was my father. He taught, by his own actions, that the more avenues one could travel during life, the more interesting life would be. His philosophy was that, when one "uses up" an activity, be it for work or play, that activity should be put aside and something else should be sought and pursued.

One of the most vivid and telling examples of his lessons on "knowing when to quit" is evidenced by the oft told story about a lady who was a professor of biology at Meredith College. This lady was not married and was usually referred to as Miss Barber, as opposed to Professor Barber. My father and I would go to Miss

Barber's house from time to time to paint or to wax floors. There came a time when Miss Barber reached an age when she was forced to retire. She had been a biology teacher for so long that her whole life seemed to be centered around, and limited to, teaching. She was so heavily involved in teaching and so enthralled by it that just a few days following retirement she purchased for herself a dozen large female dolls and placed them on the sofa in her living room. Each day she would lecture to the dolls as though they were her students in her classroom. She did not stop holding class with these dolls until she died.

Miss Barber could not quit teaching. She was so obsessed with the notion of teaching biology that her mind refused to focus upon anything else. My father concluded, and rightly so, that she was insane. He cited her case for his children's benefit, to let them know that obsession can be a dangerous limitation. Knowing when to quit is a virtue that we should all possess.

My father taught me that life was like a poker game, or some other card game where bidding is involved. In any card game, be it poker or otherwise, the best hand wins and the other hands lose—unless the best hand is misplayed. If one is holding a poor hand, that hand should be thrown back or folded. If one holds a reasonably good hand, it should either be bet on or a bid made, because the hand stands a chance of winning. In other words, one should know when to hold and know when to fold the hand that is dealt.

To experience the fulfillment of life, the value of any given situation needs to be assessed to determine whether one should get involved or get out. Where potential is evident, as in the case of a good hand of cards, pursuit of that potential should be followed.

When a matter appears to be beyond the possibility of success, it should be dropped and a different course of action sought. Knowing when to quit or to terminate that which is doomed to fail, is the way to become associated with that which is destined for success.

THIS IS MY FATHER, SHOWING THAT POVERTY CANNOT TAKE AWAY DIGNITY. IN EFFECT, HE IS SAYING, "I AM SOMEBODY! WHO ARE YOU? ARE YOU SOMEBODY TOO?"

HOW TO KEEP A CAR

For as long as I can remember, even until he died, my father owned a car. This is nothing short of remarkable, considering the extremely low economic state in which he existed. I hasten to point out, however, that he never had the joy or experience of buying or owning a new car. Many of the cars he owned were either abandoned by a previous owner, the victim of a wreck, or considered to be completely worn out. Through his own resourcefulness and ingenuity, he developed the necessary skills to restore abandoned or worn-out cars to a condition where he could extend their lives and get many more years of service from them. He learned how to replace almost any part of a car, starting with anything from a hub cap to a hood to the whole body, from a carburetor to a transmission to the whole engine. This notwithstanding, he never purchased a new part.

His primary source for automobile parts was that of two junkyards located just outside the city limits of Raleigh. In most instances, he would go to one of the junkyards, locate wrecked cars that had the part or parts he needed, remove it (or them) and then make the final purchase. The price for any part purchased from the junkyard was quite nominal; otherwise he would not have been able to afford it.

My father's mechanical abilities with cars went well beyond that of replacing parts. He could rebuild an engine. He could also restore a banged-up body. A really astounding thing to me is that when he restored the body of a car that had been wrecked, the dents were removed or smoothed out in such a way that once the car was repainted, no one could identify where they had been located. It was equally astounding that he could paint a car by hand, using brushes, and make it appear that the car had been through a professional paint shop where spray guns and sophisticated drying and buffing equipment had been used.

All the things my father learned about keeping a car, he learned on his own. He never had a day of formal mechanical training. He had the wherewithal to do whatever was necessary in order to have his own means of transportation. Needless to say, if he had pursued the business of restoring cars for others, charging a fee, he would have done well. Although he did help others frequently, he never did charge them for his service. I rather suspect that he got more by way of satisfaction that he had helped somebody than he would have gotten if he received money for what he had done.

Admittedly, neither of my brothers nor I learned how to "make a car," which was, in effect, what he was doing. However, he did teach us the simple process of "keeping a car." He showed us by his actions and preparation that he could keep the car running and presentable by doing whatever was necessary therefor. We were taught to prepare ourselves so that we would not have to depend upon anyone else.

My brothers and I also learned from my father that the only real and effective way to provide for ourselves and for those who depended upon us was to prepare ourselves by whatever means necessary, regardless of circumstances. This is not limited to providing transportation. This lesson applies to any area for which we assume responsibility. If we are to succeed in doing that which we are supposed to do, we must not only be able to "keep a car," but we also must be able to keep ourselves in a position of either knowing or learning how to help others to deal with the turmoil of life. After we are convinced that we know how to help others and not just ourselves, we must do it. "How to keep a car," then becomes, "How to drive the vehicle of life."

BUILDING A HOME FROM A HOUSE

The original house in which my mother and father lived during the early days of their marriage was a three-room shanty with running water, a kitchen sink and a toilet stool enclosed in an area just off the kitchen. There was no running water to the toilet stool. When it was used, a pan or bucket of water, obtained from the kitchen, had to be poured into the stool so that it could flow through the drainpipe. There was no other means of flushing the stool. The three rooms consisted of a living room, bedroom and kitchen—with a small area of the kitchen serving as a rest room.

By the time I was born, my father had expanded the house to five rooms, including three bedrooms, a living room and kitchen. While I was rather young, he moved the toilet stool from the kitchen area to an area just outside one of the bedrooms, still without flushing capabilities and, of course, without bathing facilities.

I was still in elementary school when we added running water to the toilet area and installed a new stool that could be flushed. Only cold water was provided, because we could not yet afford a hot water heater. Before bathroom facilities were installed, my oldest sister had gotten married and lived in a city-owned apartment that was equipped with a very nice bathroom. She and her husband were wonderfully accommodating, since many of my family kept a steady flow of activity in their bathroom.

The installation of a flushable toilet stool in our house was probably the most welcome addition that the family had received up to that time. The absence of hot water was not important enough to cause anyone to complain. Fortunately, when the toilet area was moved from the kitchen, my father had built a room sufficiently large enough to accommodate a sink and a bathtub, based on the assumption that these items would one day become available. Using my own initiative, when I was a ninth grader, I bought a bathtub and sink for the bathroom. I had obtained the money for the bathtub and sink primarily from a small accumulation I had managed to save from doing odd jobs I had performed during the year and from my summer job. In the meantime, my father was able to install a hot water heater in an area of the kitchen.

Another place where the male members of my family took baths quite frequently was at Jones' Barber Shop. The owner of the shop, Mr. Raymond Jones, was also the family barber. He had two shower stalls erected in the rear of his shop for the purpose of renting them to customers for twenty-five cents per shower. It was always a refreshing relief when my father, brothers and I could afford the luxury of a twenty-five cent shower. Mr. Jones was very proud of the fact that he was able to offer shower service to the male population of Raleigh. The service was so popular that often there would be a rather long waiting line for use of the showers. Interestingly enough, I know of no incident where complaints were ever registered by customers using the public shower facilities.

What started out as a three-room shanty in which my parents and some of their children lived, with time was transformed finally into a seven-room house with living room, dining room, kitchen, family room, three bedrooms and a full and complete bathroom. The living room, dining room and family room sometimes doubled as bedrooms. As remarkable as it seems, no outside contractor or builder was ever engaged to do any of the carpentry work, plumbing, electrical work, brick or concrete work. Each new room was added by the hands of my father and his children, except for occasional assistance from my father's brother, Uncle Jim, who was skilled in plumbing and masonry.

Of greater importance, however, was the realization that as the physical structure was being developed, inside that structure a family learned, appreciated and respected the value of love, compassion and devotion for and to each of its members. This place, where happiness was the ultimate by-product of all that had gone into its building, was a home, not just a house. The road to that happiness was not without hard times and sorrows, but the sharing of the bad with the good by all who resided in that one household attested to its transformation into that which can rightfully and properly be referred to as a home. To my family, home was more than simply a shelter. It was a place to live as brothers and sisters, mother and father, a place where love abounded. To us, one could be comfortably sheltered, but still could be homeless. We were fortunate to claim our shelter as a home. That is the way it was meant to be.

BY 1940, MY FATHER HAD DOUBLED THE SIZE OF THE HOUSE.

THE PROBLEMS OF HONESTY

Often we learn from each other by observation. At other times, we learn as a direct result of having been taught. Still, at other times, we may learn from deduction, from analogy or from an inherent or innate ability to determine the difference between realism and fantasy.

In the case of learning the true meaning of honesty, I have encountered situations that cloud the issue so drastically that I sometimes feel honesty, in a sense, does not even exist. Although I considered my father to have been an honest man, he gave me reasons to raise serious questions as to what comprised absolute honesty and indeed, if such was definable. These questions are of such magnitude, I really feel that the problems created by honesty may outweigh the virtues of honesty. My father taught me to deal with such issues and to analyze them. To me the substantiality of the problems directly associated with honesty is of great consequence.

Any comprehensive discussion of the subject of honesty must, of necessity, include such affectations as dishonesty, lying, truth, deception and ignorance. Certainly, if honesty was absolute, there would be no dishonesty, nor would there be lying, or anything else that is contrary to truth. Also, one could be totally ignorant about a given matter or situation, thinking that he/she is knowledgeable and is speaking the truth. When confronted, however, the individual is found to be, in actuality, unconsciously lying. Such an individual could be considered honest as far as behavior is concerned, but as far as principle is concerned, is totally devoid of truth.

The society in which we live, to a great extent, dictates dishonesty and lying as essential characteristics of human existence. All too often, lies are used for the purpose of denial of wrongdoing, deceiving or hiding the truth, in attempts to gain something for which the liar is not entitled and various other reasons. Lying is also frequently used as a means of avoiding embarrassment and trying to make people feel good about themselves when the truth might cause distress or despondence. How common it is to hear someone compliment another on the beauty of a performance, when, truthfully speaking, the performance was awful. The same is true when one tells another how beautiful or pretty is the clothing being worn, rather than saying that it looks ugly. So many times, children receive encouraging applause for performances that are terrible in nature. Even though the children might have performed badly, it is usual for them to be made to feel that they were wonderful by offering enthusiastic applause.   Such applause represents the sounds of lying and not the sounds of truth.

Where in today's society can a system of complete honesty be found? Certainly not in the home or within families. There is no complete system of honesty in the church, in government, in social relationships, in law and the courtroom, in medicine, in politics, in competitive sports, or in any other identifiable element of society. In too many instances, it is easier to live a lie than to live the truth. My father taught me how to identify such problems and how to express my feelings about them.

Children sometimes lie to their parents, especially if it is convenient and will keep them out of trouble. Parents lie to each other about many different things, with outside love affairs being a prime example. Husbands and wives without children also use lying as a form of deception and as a tarpaulin thrown over the truth. There are some married persons involved in outside love affairs who take the position that to be honest and disclose information about their affairs would create family and relational problems, possibly leading to breakups. Thus, honesty becomes a much greater problem to these individuals than dishonesty.

To use the word "honesty" in the same sentence with the words "government" and/or "politics" requires immediate explanation and qualification. It is highly doubtful that anyone is naive enough to believe that honesty is a prevalent characteristic of those in positions of power in government and politics. In order to become a part of government, most political aspirants appear to be willing to make promises that knowingly cannot be fulfilled. They promise the world, but deliver little— sometimes nothing.

When the President of the United States can get away with lying, simply by saying that he "misspoke," it suggests the conclusion that the higher one's position in government, the closer that individual is to infallibility. There have been instances where the political defense of presidential lying would offer support to the notion that the President of the United States should be granted, if not already entitled to, a position of infallibility. This is most often the case within the President's own staff or political party. Widespread acceptance of situations such as described, leads one to believe that for some, a state of immunity to lying can be established.

Having been involved with a number of court cases over a period of years, I have learned some very interesting things about lying and the law. Any number of times, I have been witness to the creation of positions by plaintiff's and defendant's legal counsel that bore no resemblance whatsoever to truth. If the court (judge and/or jury) accepts that which is presented, although it is totally untrue, either the prosecution or the defense suffers the consequences of lying. One of the most vivid examples of the problems of honesty regarding the court of law that I can recall comes, not from a real situation, but from a drama. The first time I ever attended a performance at the John F. Kennedy Center in Washington, DC, there was a court scene in which the defendant was testifying on his own behalf. In response to a question by the prosecution, the defendant's lawyer became very disturbed. When the defense lawyer countered, he asked the defendant what was the basis for the disturbing answer. The defendant said that he was simply telling the truth. To this the lawyer responded with great animation, "There is no place for truth in this courtroom!"

Although this was a theatrical presentation, my experience fully supports the position that, if truth is detrimental to a legal case, on either side, lawyers would prefer that it not be disclosed. On the other hand, if a fabricated position can withstand the cross-examination of the other side, it can become a determinative factor in the trial. All too often, it is much easier for one to get out of a situation by lying, than to get out by telling the truth. The old adage, "The truth will set you free," was not coined for use in the courtroom.

One could logically believe that there would be a greater practice of honesty in the church than in any other element of society. Such a logical belief is immediately destroyed, however, if one simply reads about, or becomes knowledgeable about the many acts of dishonesty that have taken place within the religious community over the past several years. Most notable is the absence of truth in the areas of homosexual practice, child molestation, extra-marital affairs and misuse of funds.

If morality were the top priority in today's world, with honesty leading the way in the parade of life, human living would be completely different from what it is now. Unfortunately, morality tends to get lost somewhere in the marching band and honesty gets drowned by the sounds of the percussion section.

AGE IS SACRED

My paternal grandmother lived to be more than one hundred years of age. I have to attribute this, at least in part, to the endearment in which she was held and treated by my father and her other son and daughters. As far as I can recall, never a week passed without my father visiting his mother and taking his children along to get to know their grandmother. When she died, some of her grandsons, myself included, served as pallbearers for her funeral.

This endearment is indicative of the awe and respect that my father offered to his elderly mother as well as to old people in general. He felt that one who had withstood and survived the trials and tribulations of time, reaching the stage of life called old age, deserved to be treated in a very special kind of way. He insisted that all of his children maintain the same kind of respect and honor for old people that he maintained himself. He viewed the attainment of old age with a serene sacredness.

In addition to my grandmother, there were several other elderly members of my family who were also treated royally. A cousin, who lived just outside Raleigh in a small town called Garner, was a favorite of my whole family. She, along with her husband and children, lived on a small farm that had many fruit trees. Included were apple, plum, pear and peach trees. Whenever we visited this cousin and her family during warm weather, usually on Sunday afternoons after church, we would all sit and talk inside the house for about an hour. After that, the children were allowed to go outside and play. If the fruit trees were bearing, we were given a free hand in eating and gathering fruit to take home. We also were allowed to play with the chickens and other harmless animals.

During cold weather, all of the visiting with this cousin and her family would take place on the inside of the house. Even then, she would always put together a gift package for us to take home at the end of the visit. The package included fruit or vegetables that she had canned during the summer plus black walnuts, pecans and meat. I sometimes felt that my father was paying for the package, because he would give her a monetary gift of a few dollars at the end of each visit. I learned eventually that he was only trying to help her financially, even though it represented a sacrifice on his part. My family loved this cousin, not just because she was kind, but because she was elderly and wise. She had earned our respect by her longevity, as well as her kindness. We cheerfully gave respect to her. My father gave us the opportunity to see families caring for each other and giving of what they had to each other.

If any one of the children in my family failed to demonstrate love and compassion for elderly members of the family, he or she was immediately in big trouble with both my father and my mother. When some disrespectful act was committed toward an older person by any of us, punishment commensurate therewith was sure to come. Seldom was such punishment necessary, however, because we knew how we were to treat the elderly. For the most part, we did not violate the accepted rules of behavior which our parents had presented to, and demanded of, us.

The position taken by my parents and the rest of my family toward the elderly was not necessarily consistent with the tenor of the time. Generally, American society provided little special consideration for the aged. Unlike some other nations, this country had not established a clear record of taking care of its older citizens. In more recent times, however, there has fortunately been some movement toward providing a better life for the elderly such as that which my parents saw as a need during their own lifetime.

Even when they reached that point in life when they could be classified themselves as elderly, my parents put forth great efforts to help others who were similarly categorized. Interestingly enough, I do not recall ever having discussed with my parents whether they felt that the responsibility for the elderly should rest with, or at least be shared with, any governmental agency. It is my belief that they felt very strongly that government really had no responsibility for persons who had outlived their direct usefulness to society. They probably felt that government had no responsibility for any individual citizen whose problems could be resolved simply by the provision of money. This was an extremely conservative point of view, but totally unlike the views of some who are involved with the administration of government today. To carry out their own beliefs, my parents never sought welfare assistance, even though their economic circumstances and level were such that they would have easily qualified for whatever assistance that might have been available. Their love and their respect for the elderly were not only symbols of concern for others, but they were also symbols of their philosophy of life.

HANDLING GRIEF

Although there may be many sources from which grief may come, the most common source, by far, is that of the loss of human life. Grief often goes well beyond the creation of feelings of sadness, and it may cause devastating effects on the human mind.

My own feelings about grief have been reached, for the most part, as a result of reflecting upon and analyzing my father's behavior in grief-filled situations. He seemed to be able to handle the loss of relatives and close friends with a type of understanding that eluded most other people that I have observed.

My belief is that he looked at such losses with a total sense of realism, concluding that there was no way available to him to restore the loss once it had occurred. He also appeared to be able to find something positive in any negative situation, even within the empty negative feelings produced by death. His approach to dealing with the grief caused by death, was that of concentrating upon the life the individual had lived and not upon the death, or loss, of the individual. For example, if someone close to him died, he would immediately begin to recall and focus upon the joyous, good and happy times and pleasant memorable experiences and the associations that he could identify as having taken place during the life of the individual who was now deceased. He promoted the fact that if the deceased had not participated in the phenomenon of living, there would have been no loss or anything else for which to be sad or sorry. Put in another way, one could never lose that which one never had. When one no longer possesses what we know as life, there should be a celebration of "what was," instead of mourning over "what is." That was the position espoused by my father.

There are those who tend to allow grief to influence, or even determine a great part of their behavior and state of mind for prolonged periods after the loss of a loved-one or close friend. This usually comes about, among other things, as a result of denial or refusal to accept the fact that life no longer exists in the body of the deceased. In the case of denial, it is relatively easy to convince one's self that human existence can continue beyond death. Mental rejection of loss becomes a psychological reality. The rejection, or denial, presents itself in many forms, including emulation, perceived communication and self-deception.

Many times, I have heard persons subconsciously address another person standing before them by using the name of a deceased individual. I have also observed persons whose behavioral characteristics have changed in such a way that they seek to emulate the behavior of deceased persons. There are times when the speech of some survivors goes through such a distinct transformation that they sound exactly like the deceased, often using the same words and phrases they think the deceased would have used. All of these are unrealized expressions of grief shown for the loss of the departed.

Guilt is another source of grief. This is one of the most difficult problems arising in the minds of some survivors. If survivors adhere to the feeling that they did not do all that they could have done in caring or providing for the deceased, the likely consequence is guilt. It is not unusual for guilt to develop in the minds of older survivors who suffer the loss of younger loved ones. For humans, the well-used expression, "only the good die young," goes far beyond just being a statement. When a young person dies, survivors may develop a level of guilt that makes them want to atone for having taken away and claimed for themselves part of the life of the one who was lost. For example, an older person may say, "Take me Lord."

It is also quite normal for younger survivors to experience the same type of guilt as older survivors, if they feel a sense of neglect in how they cared for their elderly loved ones. This is particularly true in the case of children who can, but do not provide, care for a parent or parents who succumb to death.

My father did not need the kind of counseling that so many grief-affected persons need today. He looked at death as another part of life, realizing, again, that had there been no life, there would be no death. He clearly rejected any notion that death represented the end of life, but he held firmly to the concept that death is simply and unknown extension of life.

MUSIC, DANCE AND PRAYER

The combination of music, dance and prayer may appear to be somewhat of an oddity. However, when I think of the things my father taught me in each of these areas, I feel compelled to discuss them together.

My father had no musical training, but possessed a natural ability to sing and play the piano. He could also make unusual musical sounds with his voice and with such devices as the harmonica, which we called the "juice harp." He used his hands—tapping and slapping against his legs and chest—and little pieces of wood being tapped together. He found other innovative instruments, including strips of metal, tin cans, glass bottles, cardboard and almost anything from which one can produce sounds. To add to that, he was never at a loss in composing a song spontaneously and singing it as if he had learned it from some other source. Although he did not have a great voice, his singing was always meaningful because there was a message included, whether it was an original song that he had composed spontaneously or whether it was a song composed by someone else. Singing for him was a way of expressing himself, or it was a means by which he freed his mind of troubling thoughts. The messages from his singing were not necessarily meant to be heard by others—they were for himself.

Piano playing was something that he dearly loved. The strange thing about it though, is that he could play only one series of chords with his left hand. For the most part, he even seemed to be able to play only one basic melody with his right hand. One could hear essentially the same melody in his piano playing, irrespective of the tune he should have been playing. How well he played, or what he played, however, was not the important lesson in his performance. What I learned from his piano playing and from his singing and other musical pursuits was that there is great value— therapeutic, spiritual and otherwise—in the participation in musical experiences, whether as the producer of the music, or just as the listener. Music to my father was an absolute and fundamental part of his life.

His piano playing would take on a special significance during the month of May while he worked at Meredith College. This was the month when, each year, there would be a special May Day celebration put on by the students and faculty of the college. The celebration was always held on the outside in an area called "The Grove." The Grove was like an amphitheater, with a permanent stage and space for the placement of folding chairs. The stage had to be set up with piano and scenery. The chairs had to be moved from various locations around the campus and also set up. The principal vehicle for moving the equipment to The Grove was a horse-drawn wagon. My father, of course, was a member of the crew. One of the highlights of the May Day celebration took place even before the main event occurred. This was the move of the piano from the chapel to The Grove. My father established the tradition of playing the piano while it was being carried across the campus. There were those who knew that he would be sitting on the wagon playing the piano on the day that it was to be moved. Many of them would form a viewing and listening audience along the route traveled, just as though there had been a parade taking place. The rhythm of his playing might have changed from year to year, but the tune was always the same. This did not seem to matter, because the audience never failed to show up.

My father would be pleased to know that from his love and concern for music, I have concluded that life itself is very much like a song. When one considers that songs can be short or they can be long, so can life. When one also considers that songs can be sad, they can be happy, they can be fulfilling or they can be disappointing—so can life. Songs can be the source from which come feelings of love and compassion for other living beings. Is not life itself that same source? There are songs that sometimes make no sense. Does life always make sense? Certainly those of us who live it can make no claim that life always makes sense because we are prone to do things ourselves that are nonsensical. When a requiem is sung for those who have departed from life as it is known by the living, is this not simply a song of the finality of life?

Dancing was really something special for my father. Even as he grew to be an old man, he could dance with such a high level of energy, one would be hard put to believe that someone of his age was capable of the body movements, gyrations and footwork coming from him. The only thing to stop him from dancing was death itself. As long as there was life in his body, he danced. Dancing, just like singing was an outlet for emotional expression.

Meredith College also played a role in his love for dancing. Once a year, he would organize a group of men who worked at the college to put on a cakewalk. There would be at least three competing pairs of men involved. The cakewalk was held in the dining hall, and the students and faculty would gather together to watch the men dance from one end of the hall to the other. A committee of judges was formed from the faculty to determine the winning pair. The prizes for winning the cakewalk included a special cake, baked by one of the cooks who worked in the kitchen of the college, and a sum of money that had been collected as donations from those who attended the event. All the participants were dressed in original costumes, prepared for the cakewalk. The judges took into consideration the originality of the costumes in deciding on the winners.

Cakewalk time was a night of fun for many people, especially for the participants. For as long as I can remember, my father and his partner were first place winners, until the last cakewalk in which he participated. I do believe that he decided to forget about the cakewalk when the competition got too strong. As I recall, the last winner was a pair of men that included the cook that baked the cake. Admittedly, the winning pair was much younger than my father and his partner, so age might have been a factor, even though the losers put on a stellar performance. What happened is that my father had won for so long that he could not cope with the thought of losing. Therefore, he let the whole thing die.

How does prayer come into this discussion? My father saw prayer as an art form, the same way he viewed music and dance. He considered prayer as a means of relieving himself of frustration and emotional trauma. If he did not sing to get relief, or if he did not dance to get relief, he would pray. He might even combine the three, for there were times when he would dance while singing a song that was really a prayer. For him, praying was an essential for living. At night, he would not go to bed before he got on his knees and prayed. It made no difference how tired he might be or how late it was, his final act before retiring at night was that of praying on his knees. Although he did not insist on his children doing the same thing, most of them followed his lead. Time probably changed the attitude of some of the children as far as getting on their knees was concerned, but I do not believe that any one of the ten would ever think about going to sleep without praying.

Whenever my father had a need that he could not satisfy by doing whatever was necessary himself, he looked to prayer as the means by which the need could be met. He felt that the Lord God Almighty was always available to aid and assist him in his needs. He really had no compunction about calling upon God for anything he thought was a reasonable need. If his prayer was not answered immediately, he was not ever discouraged, because he thought that God would respond to his requests at some point in time. Although he prayed in his own interest, he also prayed in praise and glorification of God. I believe that he thought God would give him more attention if his prayers showed God how much he cared and how much he respected God's power.

The ability to perform music, to dance and to pray may very well have been considered by my father as his three most important virtues. Whereas these talents may not be characterized as virtues by everyone, there was no question as to my father's categorization of them. These three represented his most cherished set of virtues. I would never think of them in any other terms.

THE POWER OF THE KNEES

As I have indicated, my father would not go to bed at night without getting down on his knees to pray. Although his prayers were not audible to those of us who liked to watch him pray, all kinds of things entered our minds as to what he might be saying. We did know, however, that his state of mind was always good when he arose.

Using my imagination and my words, but knowing his approach to life, I have listed some things that might be representative of his prayer and praying. If he had shared what happened to him as he prayed, I believe that his many actions and reactions would have been expressed in a similar manner. I feel strongly that both the content of his faith in prayer and his unyielding trust in the power of the knees are depicted. What might he have said? I think it would have gone like this:

1. *I went down praying and got up praising.*

2. *I went down feeling like I was on my last leg and on the way out, but I got up with a new burst of energy, feeling as if I was just getting started.*

3. *I went down feeling unworthy and I cried out, "Father, I am not worthy that Thou shouldst enter under my roof. Speak but the word and my soul shall be healed." As I knelt there, I could hear the voice of Jesus saying, "You have been made worthy and you should receive the bread and wine that represent both my body and my blood, as often as you can. Do this in remembrance of me." When I got up, I knew that I had already been redeemed and that my redemption would be confirmed all over again every time I took Holy Communion.*

4. *I slumped down on my knees feeling tired, weak and listless, and I shared these feelings with the Lord in the best way I knew how. When I got up, my body felt as if I had received a blood transfusion. I was stunned when I realized that the blood I had received was the blood of Jesus, and my body had not rejected it. I felt like Jesus had changed my blood type so that it was the same as His. As the blood of Jesus flowed through my arteries and my veins, I began to take on a new attitude. My mind was flooded with thoughts of how I could make myself*

deserving of this transformation that came from the transfusion. Evidently, Jesus decided to interrupt my thoughts and let me know that all I needed to do was to let others know about praying and to help them understand the power that comes from prayer. He told me to share the good news of His presence within me with those around me. Let them know, in no uncertain terms, that they too are targets of His love, and that his presence is also forever within them.

5. *When I got down on my knees, I was having a hard time seeing, but when I arose, I felt as though I was wearing a new pair of eye glasses. The lenses had been ground and polished on the whetstone of holiness. Now there was nothing that I could not see, for God had given me new vision. It had come from the power generated by prayer, the power of the knees. God allowed me to see easily what he meant when He said, "I am the way, the truth and the light." For me, that light was now shining brightly, where before there was only darkness. Mine eyes had seen the glory of the coming of The Lord!*

6. *When I went down on my knees, I was not sure whether I could contact the Lord on my own. When I got up, I realized that I had been talking on a direct line to Jesus. It was not necessary to go through an operator, nor was it necessary to dial "information." I did not even have to look up the number or an area code to place the*

call. God said, "If you know the prayer code, you know how to reach Me." That code had come to me through the power of the knees.

7. *When I went down, I was in a state of agony. When I came up, I was in a state of ecstasy.*

8. *When I went down, sorrow and sadness engulfed me. When I got up, joy, happiness and gladness had taken over.*

9. *When I got down on my knees to pray, I was being haunted by the devil. When I arose, I was walking hand-in-hand with The Lord. The devil was nowhere to be found. He was chased away by the power of The Almighty. With God at my side, I was no longer afraid of that demon known as the devil. It was too late for him to have any influence on me. The power of the knees had removed him completely.*

10. *When I got down on my knees to pray, my heart was feeling as though it wasn't beating properly. While I was there, I felt the "stethoscope of Jesus" pressing on my chest, and I knew that my divine cardiologist listened to my heartbeat and declared me to be "fit as a fiddle." What a sobering thought it was to learn that Jesus is the connecting link between the knees and the heart, with prayer being the switch that activates the connection.*

11. *All during the day, I had been thinking about angels. Even as I was getting ready for bed,*

my mind would not free itself from thoughts relating to angels. As I descended to my knees and thanked God for the day and for all the things He had done for me, I began to petition Him, asking Him to help me get a better understanding of what being an angel is all about. I explained that it was difficult for me to visualize human-like bodies with wings sticking out from their backs and shoulders, flying around like birds. I asked for help in understanding whether everyone who enters the Kingdom of Heaven is immediately issued a set of wings. I also asked if angels are invisible beings that come back and fly around the earth, or are their flights limited to the Heavenly Kingdom. I wanted to know, as well, if an angel is simply a messenger for the Lord, or are angels responsible for other things? Evidently, God had been listening to me and decided that He had heard enough of my questions. All of a sudden, I felt as though there was an answering machine in my head and an incoming message was being received, not directly from the Lord, but from an Angel of the Lord. I could hear the voice of the angel saying, "This message is for the inquisitor who seems to be confused about angels. You should know that to be an angel does not mean that one necessarily has to possess physical wings. To be an angel does not mean that a human being has to die and go to heaven. To be an angel means that one must first believe in God, The Father Almighty, creator of heaven and earth. To be an angel, one must live in accordance with the will of God.

Angels reside both in heaven and on earth. To be an angel is to do unto others as you would have them do unto you. To be an angel is to feed the hungry, to clothe the naked, to provide comfort for the distressed and to house the homeless. You should stop thinking and worrying about what angels are like and start doing the things that angels do. In that way, you can demonstrate for others what angels are like, and others will not have to raise all the questions that you have raised in your own mind. They will know that you are acting like an angel. End of message!" When I got up from my knees, I began to realize that the questions I had raised about angels in my mind had been planted there by God. The answers to these questions were to make me fully aware that I needed to make some serious changes in the way I live my life on earth. I had been told, in clear terms, that the wings of angels are designed for givers, not for receivers. For me to qualify for my earthly wings, I had to transform my life by eliminating all self-centered behavior and actions. I needed to start using my time to help carry out the work of the Lord, just as the Angels of the Lord carry out that work. Again, my knees proved to be the solution to my problems, and because of the power of my knees, all of my questions about angels had been answered.

12. *As I eased down on my knees, I thought I would be able to negotiate with God, offering to do certain things for Him if He would do certain things for me. It suddenly became apparent to*

me that I had no power with which to negotiate with the Lord. I thought about Moses on Mount Sinai who could not and did not tell the Lord what to write on the tablets of stone. Rather, the Lord told Moses what to write, and there he received the wording of the Ten Commandments. Moses did not try to negotiate changes in the wording. He knew that he was being commanded to do the work of the Lord. I asked myself what makes me think that the Lord wants to negotiate with me. I concluded that I had better understand what the power of God is all about, and I had better keep in mind what had been etched on those two tablets of stone, so that I could keep and follow those commandments just as Moses and the other people of the world had been directed. When I got up, I knew that something had to change in the way I looked at myself from within.

13. *When I went down on my knees, I was holding a bunch of yellow dandelions that made me sneeze. As I communicated with the Lord, praising Him and asking for help, while still clinging to those dandelions in my hand, I knew that something good was happening to me. The sneezing had gone away. When I arose, I was holding a bouquet of roses, gardenias and orchids. The aroma convinced me that the Lord had been involved in this transformation of wild, weedy flowers into some of the most fragrant species of them all. I was absolutely certain then, the Lord was also able to*

transform a meaningless life into a life of glory, when the power of the knees was used as the basis for the change.

14. *For some unknown reason, I knelt down to thank God for the fact that I was in the good hands of the Allstate Insurance Company. It did not take long for me to forget that Allstate even existed, for God had lifted me up on eagle's wings and He was holding me in the palm of His hand. What a difference a hand can make, if that hand is the Hand of God.*

15. *For some strange reason, I got down on my knees to find out if the Lord would listen to ghetto and street language. I started off by saying, "Lord, things need to be 'mo better' if I'm gonna be the kind of 'badd Christian' that I think 'y'all' want me to be. I need some 'bumpin rags,' some 'slick wheels' and a pocket fulla 'green bread' to help me do unto udders as dey would do unto me." I was shocked when all of a sudden, I heard the Lord say, "Yo brudder man, dere ain't no need for me to give you all dis stuff you're asking for. I want you to share whatever you got now with the other chillun who got less than you. Don't try to con me and make me feel guilty for not giving a lot of stuff, you know. You got enough stuff already to be able to hep somebody else. Be thankful for what you have now and make somebody else thankful that you gave them a piece of the pie that I baked for you when I put life in that body you carry*

*around from day to day. Come on brudder
man, it's time to 'chill out' on dis 'askin gig' and
git into the 'givin and sharing thang.' Put a
CD in your head and listen to the rap of love
and understanding. Yo day will come. Be cool!"
When I got up, I was embarrassed, but I knew
what I had to do. I had to get myself together
and start following the teachings of Jesus far
more closely than I ever had before. The power
of my knees had put the power of my mind to
shame.*

16. *As I went down on my knees, I felt as though I
was both grounded and stranded. I had the
feeling that I was unable to move my body or
my mind to a place or position of comfort. As
usual, I asked the Lord what could I do to help
myself and to change the situation. All of a
sudden, my mind seemed to have become
reactivated, and I felt that I was now sitting on
the roadside of redemption. Up rolled God's
limousine of love. It was equipped with a
flashing message board, sending words of
encouragement and wisdom. Now I know how
Moses felt when he received those commanding
words of the Lord while on that mountain top.
When the door of the limousine opened, I
thought it was time for me to get inside, but a
new flashing message appeared, which read,
"You are not to board this vehicle, but you are
directed to put down a deposit for the purchase
of a similar vehicle for yourself by giving up
this selfish search for comfort and start to
dedicate your energies and efforts towards*

comforting others who are in far greater need than you. Each time you do something good for someone else, you will have made another payment on your own limousine. The number of payments you have to make will be determined by the number of unselfish deeds that you do." God's limousine than took off. When I got up, I felt that I was already in position to move or go anywhere I chose. I had the feeling that God had not only offered me a luxury car, but that He had offered to be my chauffeur. Prayer is a powerful thing!

The power of the knees can be shown in strange ways sometimes. My father was a living testimony of the power of the knees. He knew that the quality of life may be determined by the quantity of prayer. Furthermore, he understood that the quantity of life may very well be determined by the quality of prayer. He taught me that to lose one's self in prayer is to lose one's self in the power of God.

WHAT KIND OF CHRISTIAN ARE YOU?

There are times when the inquisitive nature of my father's mind invades my own mind. I begin to ask myself questions that I truly believe he would have asked himself or would have asked anybody else. Certainly, one of those questions would have been, "What kind of Christian am I? More importantly, "What kind of Christian are you?" After asking the question, he would have continued the process with a series of sub-questions. Some of the sub-questions and comments that would have followed the basic question would be as follows:

1. Are you a PEW CHRISTIAN or a DO CHRISTIAN? In other words, are you one who attends church on Sunday morning simply to sit in a pew and listen to others preach, pray, sing

and worship?   Or are you one who works from day to day in trying to influence the lives of others in such a way that living is better? PEW Christians see church as a means of helping themselves and as a basis for religious self-satisfaction.   Those who can be called, DO Christians, see church as the headquarters for determining how best to get busy and interact positively with the family of God, doing unto others and for others as they would have others do unto and for themselves.

2. Are you a TABLOID-READING CHRISTIAN or a BIBLE-READING CHRISTIAN? All too often, curiosity determines what one reads. The exciting headlines on tabloids can cause one to get carried away about what someone else has done that is not in harmony with what one supposedly should have done. True Christians get far more excited when they read the Holy Bible and learn what the word of God is all about.

3. Are you a RIDING CHRISTIAN or a DRIVING CHRISTIAN? If the Christian simply sits back and depends upon others for transportation through the journey of life, the route traveled could lead to an unwanted destination. However, if the Christian is willing and able to serve as the driver or chauffeur for this journey, the stages and end points of life can and will be reached. Being able to read and follow the maps of life's tours, trips and cruises in a way that God would have us do is the way to lay claim to true Christianity. Riding through life will not bring

the benefits, payments and the tips that driving through life will bring.

4. Are you a FLOATING CHRISTIAN or a SWIMMING CHRISTIAN? The Christian who gets into the water just to float around is not like the Christian who gets into the water to swim. The FLOATING Christian lets the water determine the direction taken. The SWIMMING Christian makes that determination. If a fellow Christian were in danger of drowning, the FLOATING Christian would not be able to help and/or save. Conversely, the SWIMMING Christian could move to the site of the endangered Christian and rescue him or her.

5. Are you a RECEIVING CHRISTIAN or a GIVING CHRISTIAN? The importance of giving versus receiving can be expressed from a numerical standpoint. The number of times the word "give" appears in the Holy Bible dwarfs the number of times the word "receive" appears. "Give" appears in the Bible approximately 800 times. "Receive" is there less than 200 times. On this basis, giving is more than four times more important than receiving. Even comparing the number of times "giving" and "receiving" are used, twenty-nine to seven respectively, it is again four times as many uses. Real Christians know that they automatically receive from God the things they need, either directly or indirectly. Thus they should share these blessings with others so that they can be worthy of the title, GIVING Christians.

6. Are you an ARMS-CROSSED CHRISTIAN or a HAND-WAVING CHRISTIAN? The feelings of Christianity can be expressed in many different ways. There are those who feel that waving their hands during a church service in response to music, the reading of a Bible passage, or to the spoken word is the best way to let God know that they are participating, as Christians, in His worship and praise. They feel that to sit motionless is to make a statement of disinterest and non-participation. Some would say that ARMS-CROSSED Christians cannot compare with HAND-WAVING Christians. They even would contend that HAND-WAVING Christians are waving their hands at God and that God is responding by waving back at them.

7. Are you a SCARED CHRISTIAN or a BRAVE CHRISTIAN? Some people call themselves Christians, yet they never share that information with others. Sometimes there is fear that if a Christian talks to a non-Christian about Christianity, the Christian will be looked upon as a wimp. Thus, the "wimp" becomes scared to advertise his or her faith in the Living God. The BRAVE Christian is ever mindful of the fact that faith is what keeps him or her going and that faith needs to be made known to others who do not realize its value. There is no fear in the BRAVE Christian when it comes to talking about God. Therefore, this type of Christian also can be classified as a TALKING Christian and not a SILENT Christian.

8. Are you an IDLE CHRISTIAN or an ACTIVE CHRISTIAN? From time-to-time one finds Christians who tend to carry their Christianity in their minds and do not exert any physical energy in bringing their beliefs to bear upon others. Those who fail to share and spread the Good News of the coming of Jesus Christ as the Savior of the world are not living their lives in the best way. God would have all Christian men, women and children constantly and continually teach the simple message that "He is the way, the truth and the life." Idleness is not an acceptable aspect of Christianity.

9. Are you a SILENT CHRISTIAN or a SINGING ~ DANCING ~ NOISY CHRISTIAN? According to Psalms 149:1-3:

> "Praise ye the Lord. Sing unto the Lord a new song, and his praise in the congregation of saints. Let Israel rejoice in him that made him: let the children of Zion be joyful in their King. Let them praise his name in the dance: let them sing praises unto him with the timbrel and harp."

Following this, Psalms 150:3-6 reads:

> "Praise him with the sound of the trumpet: praise him with the psaltery and harp. Praise him with the timbrel and dance: praise him with stringed instruments and organs. Praise him upon the loud cymbals: praise him upon the high sounding cymbals. Let every thing that hath breath praise the Lord. Praise ye the Lord."

With this kind of direction coming from the Holy Bible, how can good Christians keep their mouths shut and their instruments silent?

10. Are you a DOUBTING CHRISTIAN or a BELIEVING CHRISTIAN? Sometimes, there are those who would have others think that they are deeply into Christianity, while at the same time, they show no real seriousness about the belief that "all things are possible if you only believe." The housing of doubts in one's mind as to whether or not God has the capabilities to satisfy all needs, is tantamount to saying that "God is not omnipotent." The BELIEVING Christian carries no such thoughts. The BELIEVING Christian spends his or her time dwelling on the positive aspects of Christianity and finds no time to develop doubts.

11. Are you a WALKING CHRISTIAN or a RUNNING CHRISTIAN? If a Christian walks a mile, while another runs four miles during the same period of time, the runner has certainly covered far more territory than the walker. If the purpose of the walking and the running is to move about so that lives can be helped and service can be rendered, the WALKING Christian will not have been able to touch nearly as many lives as would have the RUNNING Christian. The practice of Christianity should not be done in the walking mode, but in the running mode.

12. Are you an EATING CHRISTIAN or a FEEDING (PROVIDING) CHRISTIAN? The Christian who is more interested in consuming food than

providing it is living inconsistently with the way that God desires us to live. PROVIDING Christians are the kind that God likes to see. Perhaps the most vivid example of eating versus feeding comes from Jesus Christ when, according to the Book of Matthew, he took two loaves of bread and two fishes, and miraculously fed multitudes of people. He was not about to let the people go hungry. Christians are expected to feed the hungry, not only those who are hungry for physical food, but also those who are hungry for the Word of the Lord.

13. Are you a GRUMPY CHRISTIAN or a PLEASANT CHRISTIAN? Those who fuss and frown most of the time are not presenting themselves as Christians should. There should be a sweetness on the face of Christians, not a sour countenance. There should be signs of happiness, not expressions of unhappiness. Hatred within the family of God is an unacceptable characteristic. Love and compassion are two of the most important elements of Christian living.

14. Are you an UNSAVED CHRISTIAN or a SAVED CHRISTIAN? Many factors must be taken into consideration in trying to conclude whether one is saved or unsaved. Among others, the state of honesty and/or dishonesty must be determined. The Christian who abides in honesty qualifies as a recipient of God's saving grace to a far greater extent than does the Christian who abides in dishonesty. The Christian who stands

up for God, rather than hiding his or her beliefs, is following the path that leads to being saved. The cleanliness of one's living is the fundamental determinant in deciding whether one is saved or unsaved. Cleanliness can come even after one has lived with dirt, since forgiveness abounds. Even the unsaved can be transformed into the saved, if the transformation and transition are sought and accepted.

15. Are you a HALLOWEEN CHRISTIAN or a CHRISTMAS CHRISTIAN? If one is a HALLOWEEN Christian, that individual probably moves about his or her neighborhood one evening of the year seeking treats from anyone who will provide them, but threatening to play tricks on anyone who will not give up treats. If the individual is a CHRISTMAS Christian, he or she will go about the neighborhood exclaiming the glory and wonderment of the birth of "Sweet Little Jesus Boy," the one who was sent to the earth to save the humankind from sin and destruction. The HALLOWEEN Christian goes back home and begins to consume the treats that were collected. The CHRISTMAS Christian goes back home and begins to work out new ways to spread the word of God. The CHRISTMAS Christian will likely decide to become a THANKSGIVING Christian, an EASTER Christian, or better still, a YEAR-ROUND CHRISTIAN.

How does one decide what kind of Christian he or she is? It all depends upon how he or she lives. To be a

Christian commensurate with the will of God, one would have to live a life of goodness, caring, sharing and loving. My father was this way. He devoted his life to being a Christian man, fully in all aspects. If one adheres to the messages and requirements of the Holy Scriptures, including the Ten Commandments, as he did, there is no question as to what kind of Christian the individual is—a GOOD CHRISTIAN.

WHAT DO WE SHOUT ABOUT?

There was a time during my early years when my   father would discuss shouting in the church with his children. He would also talk about shouting at prayer meetings on Wednesday evenings.

Today, most people talk about shouting from an entirely different perspective--all too often without even thinking about the church. Many young people of today would probably be completely baffled by a strong and dynamic shouting session at a church service. Admittedly, there are some exceptions to what I am writing here. Certain Baptist and Pentecostal churches, as well as The House of Prayer and a few other denominations still believe in the expression of spiritual emotion through shouting.

At First Baptist Church in Raleigh, which our family attended, shouting was very much a part of the Sunday morning worship service. There was one lady in particular, whose name I shall now call "Sister Mary," who appeared to be the chief "shouter."

Sister Mary could have easily been labeled as the supervisor, the coach, or even the manager of shouting. Any one of these names would have been appropriate. For the first thirty minutes or so the service would proceed without interruption, except for people saying "Amen," whenever something was said or sung with which there was strong agreement and a desire to react to the feelings experienced. When the pastor was well into his sermon, Sister Mary, as if by some divine signal, would begin jumping up from the pew, dancing a few steps and melodiously saying, "Hallelujah, praise the Lord." When this happened, the pastor would raise the volume of his voice. By the time he ended his sermon, he and Sister Mary would have coordinated their performances in such a way that it appeared as though they not only were following a prepared script, but that they also had rehearsed it as well. Other people sitting near Sister Mary would join her as she reached the top of her shouting spree. However, she was always the first to start shouting and the last to finish.

Having observed, and I must confess enjoyed, Sister Mary's shouting for many years, I began to ask myself the question, "Just what was she shouting about?" Was she shouting about God's gift of good health, including the very energy God had given her to carry out her shouting? Although she was not a woman of great means, I believe that she was highly appreciative for what she had. She credited God for giving her whatever she possessed, and she wanted her brothers and sisters to know that shouting was one way of losing herself in Christ, the Giver. I believe she was also saying to the church that she had shouted on past Sundays and she would keep on doing it every Sunday, as long as God would give her the strength to continue.

Perhaps there is yet another reason for Sister Mary's shouting. She may have been conveying the message that the church had waited long enough without recognizing and acknowledging the presence of Jesus Christ in its midst. She was more likely chiding the congregation and telling the people that the time had come to say, "Hello Jesus! Welcome to First Baptist Church. Although we knew that you were here all along, we did not welcome you the way you deserved to be welcomed. We now want you to know how much your presence is appreciated."

The pastor's reaction to Sister Mary strongly suggested that he was waiting for her signal announcing formally the presence, if not the arrival, of Jesus as a participant in the service. When she got going, the service would always take on an entirely new dimension.

There are those who would say that Sister Mary simply "Got happy" during the service, but I think that she was already happy when she came to the church. Maybe her shouting actually provided another opportunity to let those around her know just how happy she was.

By the way, Sister Mary had some moves and dance steps that could rival any Reggae or other step with which there is current familiarity. The truth is that most of the dance steps done today, including "The Electric Slide," were created right there in First Baptist Church by Sister Mary and her shouting line. It is too bad that credit was never given to her and others like her for their contributions.

The gospel singer and preacher, Shirley Caesar, sings a rousing song entitled, "Shouting John." Those who are familiar with this song know that John was not appreciated by his own church because he could not keep from shouting. The church sent a delegation to John's home to inform him that if he did not stop interrupting the Sunday morning service with his shouting, he would have to leave the church. John's response was that he had something to shout about, and he was not about to stop doing it. He showed the delegation all of the land he owned and the house that stood on it. He told them about his drug-free children and how God had been so good to him that shouting was but a small way to let God know how thankful he was. John got so carried away, he started shouting even as the delegation stood, watched and listened. He started singing, "I feel, I feel like praising God," and the level of his spiritual emotions rose higher and higher. He became so wrapped up in his shouting, the members of the delegation soon forgot why they had come to see him in the first place. It was not long before all of them had gotten so moved by the spirit shown by John that they were shouting just as hard as was he.

Unlike Sister Mary, John had a lot of material things, as well as other blessings for which he wanted God to know he would not have, were it not for the goodness of God. His purpose for shouting, however, was exactly the same as that of Sister Mary. Both of them wanted God to know that their thanks and praise were so strong, they had to be expressed in a special way, and that way was through shouting.

Shouting, as it is generally known today, does not necessarily relate to thanking and praising God. I heard a preacher say one time, that if he had reached a weak point in his sermon, he would start shouting loudly in order to regain or keep the attention of the congregation. Still another preacher said that he would always start his sermons in a shouting fashion so that he could get the attention of his congregation early. He would back off after a few minutes, but would start shouting all over again if he sensed that attention was waning. Perhaps a better word for what these preachers were talking about is "screaming." What they really meant was that, to them, loudness was a major factor in their preaching. It appears that shouting today could be expressed as a measure of loudness.

My wife and I sang in a certain church choir for many years, learning early on that the congregation would applaud the choir only if an anthem or other musical selection ended loudly. The rendition could have been very poor, but if the loud volume was there, so was the applause. The most beautiful of anthems could be sung quietly and softly, but never do I remember the choir being applauded for such.

Think about radio and television. For the most part, the sound of commercials is louder than the sound on regular programming. This obviously is supposed to bring attention of the listeners or viewers to the product being advertised. In other words, shouting, or high volume, is expected to help sell products.

Consider politicians. What do they shout about? During campaigns, candidates seem to shout either about what their opponents have not done that should have been done or about what their opponents have done that should not have been done. Seldom do they shout about what they themselves can and will do to make life better for the populace.

There is a tendency, on the part of most people, to speak louder when they are extremely happy or extremely upset than at other times. Is that kind of feeling a cause for shouting? Do most people plan their shouting as did Sister Mary and Shouting John, or do most people shout when it is appropriate? I honestly believe that people shout more than they realize. However, I am not certain that they always shout about the right things. According to the Webster's New World Dictionary, a shout is, "...a loud cry, as one expressing joy, triumph, fear, or the like." It is also, "A loud and sudden outcry or uproar." If these definitions are considered in connection with the question of, "What do we shout about," let us take a look at a few areas where individual questions should be asked about shouting, such as:

1. Do I shout about the menacing drug and smoking problems that are continuing to invade the lives of God's children, both young and old? Am I turning up the volume on the solution knob in an attempt to deal with this tragedy?

2. Am I shouting about the mounting teenage pregnancy problems that need so desperately to be dealt with

by those who are in position to make a difference? Is my voice being heard, or am I turning down the volume so that I can pretend that the problems are not real?

3. What about the AIDS problem? Am I shouting in any way to let my concerns be known, or am I leaving the problem to others for their solution? Isn't there something I can contribute to ease the situation?

4. What about Black children who have to face societal biases and plain old racist acts to which most other children are not subjected? Am I shouting about the need to make special provisions for these children so that they will be able to succeed in an oft times unfriendly and even hostile environment? Do I sometimes feel like praising, praising God like Shouting John, because God gave me the blessings that flow from having helped somebody? Or, did I fail to help somebody?

5. Am I shouting about the serious problems of intergenerational communication? Am I trying to create a setting whereby young people can be understood by older people and where older people can be understood by younger people? Are there generational languages that have developed over time? If so, am I shouting about the essentiality of bringing these languages together?

The place for shouting is no longer the church alone. The place for shouting is everywhere. When we reach the point where we can truthfully say, "We are like Sister Mary or we are like Shouting John because we can praise God for what He has caused us to do and what He has caused us to be," we will then know what we are shouting about.

HOW TO STAY YOUNG

Although my father was seventy years old when he died, he always was a young man. He would never let himself grow old. Age to him was nothing more than a figment of the imagination. I sincerely believe that he thought that the retention of youth was simply a by-product of interaction with young people. Not once in his life did he shy away from associating with children. Until the day he died, he played with children and did the things that children do, not because he had a childish mind, but because he maintained a child-like heart. His love for children was representative of love for living.

His competitive spirit notwithstanding, he taught his children how to play games both for mental and for physical exercise. One of his favorites was softball. He taught his children how to hit, catch, pitch and run bases. One of my brothers became a star softball pitcher and was sought after by many of the local softball teams. This came about because of my father's teaching. If my brother had not had the close guidance and tutoring of my father, I am certain that his skills would not have been developed to the extent that they were.

An incident that stands out in my mind is one that occurred when my father was about sixty-nine years of age. One Friday afternoon, my wife and I went to Raleigh to spend the weekend with my mother and father. As we arrived in the neighborhood where my parents' house was located, we saw a group of people playing baseball in a field close by. Not knowing who was involved in the game, we nonetheless decided to stop and say hello to whomever we might recognize. We were certain that there had to be someone in the game that we knew.

Sure enough, we recognized almost everyone we saw. To our great surprise, behind home plate, wearing a chest protector and mask, with his cap turned backwards, kneeling and waiting for the pitcher to throw the ball, was my sixty-nine year old father. Until my wife and I arrived, there could not have been another person on the field older than seventeen. Most of the players were young teenagers. We greeted my father and the others and stayed to watch the game for quite a long time. We saw him come to bat, get a hit and run the bases just as fast as the youngsters with whom he was playing. It was truly an amazing sight to see this young old man having as much fun as anyone else in the game and loving every minute of it. My wife and I were convinced from that moment on of the irrelevance of age in determining human behavior.

According to my father's philosophy, you stay young if you believe that you are young. Let nothing or no one convince you otherwise. If we are to remain young, then we should interact with others who are young— namely, the children of the world.

SENSIBLE SAYINGS THAT MAKE NO SENSE

The key to communicating with my father was accuracy. Grammar was not nearly as important to him as was the accuracy of thought. This concern for accuracy of thought had a major influence upon how members of my family communicate. As a consequence of my own concerns for accuracy of thought and speech, I tend to analyze everything that is said to me, or that I hear or read. I believe my father did the same. The difference in his approach and mine, however, is that I include the grammatical analysis.

There are widely used expressions or sayings that develop in various cultures. Some are peculiar to certain geographic areas, and some appear to be universally acceptable. Most of these sayings have meanings that are easily and immediately understood, based upon familiarity and usage. If, however, one looks at the literal meanings of the types of sayings to which I refer, one would find that they make no journalistic sense. My father has clearly influenced my thinking on this subject. Here are some examples:

I WAS SCARED TO DEATH - How ordinary it is to hear a living person say that someone or something "scared me to death." Seldom does anyone raise questions about the statement, because of its acceptance as a declaration of an extreme level of fear that has been experienced. My father would not use such a statement. Being frightened to a mind-boggling state is one thing, but literally being scared to death is something else. If one should be so unfortunate as to have been scared to death, there could no longer be vocal transmission from that individual, as far as is known. It is difficult to imagine a dead person saying that he or she is dead because of having been scared into that state.

I LAUGHED MY HEART OUT - There are few things more satisfying than a hearty laugh. But even though the phrase is suggestive, it cannot be true in a literal sense and would therefore be considered nonsensical by my father.

I CRIED MY HEART OUT - Just as it is impossible to laugh one's heart out, it is also impossible for one to cry one's heart out. Yet, it is not uncommon to hear an individual express sadness, disappointment or unhappiness by the use of this phrase. You would not hear it from my father!

A ROLLING STONE GATHERS NO MOSS - For many, this statement is considered to be profound.

However, with the clarity instilled in me by my father, I see this phrase quite differently. Some situations evidence a complete refutation of the statement. For instance, if a stone is dipped or immersed in a substance such as super glue and rolled across moss before the glue dries, some of the moss will certainly adhere to it. If a stone is wrapped in adhesive tape or Velcro, with the adhesive portion on the outside, it would also gather some of the moss. By contrast, a completely motionless stone will gather no moss, if it is in a position where no moss is present or where no moss can grow. A stationary stone in an arid desert could rest there for centuries and still gather no moss. Thus, the expression, "A rolling stone gathers no moss," is inaccurate and makes no sense unless all identifiable circumstances are taken into consideration.

A WHOLE NOTHER SUBJECT - Every time I hear someone respond to a question by saying, "That's a whole nother subject," I cringe and wince and laugh at the same time. I know full well that the individual is attempting to say, "It's another whole subject," but I am amazed at the frequency of use of the non-grammatical form. I hear it on television, I hear it on radio and I hear it in ordinary conversation far more than I should. My penchant for grammatical accuracy is an extension of my father's teaching.

THE LORD WILLING AND THE CREEK DON'T RISE - An old expression of hope and promise that something will be accomplished at a certain time or on a certain date in the future, or that someone will return to a particular place at a given time is embodied in this phrase. I like the first part that acknowledges unbounded faith and confidence in the will of God—so would have my father. However, he also believed that with the Lord's blessing he was master of his fate and not dependent upon the possibility that a creek might rise and jeopardize the whole thing. He also felt that fate was not dependent upon any other physical manifestation. Suffice it to say, rising creeks seldom determine whether or not an event will happen.

I'M BURNING UP - How common it is to hear a person who is uncomfortable because of heat, or is suffering from the effects of hot weather say, "I'm burning up." Obviously, unless one has been set on fire, or is inside an oven, kiln or other heat producing device, it is highly unlikely that the individual is really burning up. Even if a person dies from a heat stroke, that person will not have burned up. Has the body turned to ashes? Of course not! My father would cringe at this kind of statement about heat as well as the next one about cold.

I'M FREEZING - It is possible for a person to incur frostbite or to endure freezing certain bodily organs for surgical purposes (and then thawing them). However, for one to contend that he or she is freezing because of uncomfortably cold weather, or because improper clothing might be worn, is suggestive of extremity. If an individual really is freezing and nothing is done quickly to stop the process, the odds of surviving are slim indeed. Seldom does one who is experiencing temperatures at or below the freezing point of water (thirty-two degrees Fahrenheit or zero degrees Celsius) also experience literal freezing of his or her body. Normally, there is little or no accuracy that can be associated with the assertion that, "I'm freezing."

HE IS HIGH AS A KITE - To describe a male who is intoxicated, or just plain drunk, as being "high as a kite," would either have no meaning to one who is unfamiliar with the expression, or it would simply lead to confusion. When a kite is connected with height, an assumption is made that the kite is in the air, attached to a cord and flying well above ground level. Although there may be some illogical comparison of kites with bungee jumping, parachuting, or other mechanically assisted flying processes, there is no logical connection between a kite and a male affected by alcohol. From another perspective, a kite does not even have to be in the air at all. It could be on the ground, on a table, on the floor, in one's hand, or at any other ground-level position. The kite may not be high at all. So what is the literal comparison between a drunken male and a kite? My father would feel that it really makes no sense to say that someone is "high as a kite," unless a clarifying explanation is included with this statement.

HAPPY BIRTHDAY — An in-depth analysis of the term, "Happy Birthday," reveals that it makes very little literal sense. In truth, the day on which one is born is a one-time occurrence in life. Thus, a birthday is a singular event, taking place in one particular year and never again. The real meaning of this phrase would be more clearly delineated as "Happy Birthday Anniversary." Even if this approach were used, it would not be chronologically accurate, unless periodic adjustments were made. Consider, for example, one who was born on June 1, 1950. Each year, on the first day of June thereafter, the birthday anniversary would be celebrated. However, since a full year is comprised of three hundred sixty-five and one-fourth days, the date of the birthday anniversary should be increased by one day every four years. At age four, the celebration should have been on June 2nd. At age eight, it should have been on June 3rd. When the individual reached the age of forty in 1990, ten days should have been added to the original birth date, thus causing the anniversary to be celebrated properly on June 11, 1990. Otherwise, the anniversary celebration date would be incorrect. The same thinking applies to wedding anniversary celebrations and any other annually celebrated event.

HE'S AS OLD AS METHUSELAH — For one to be accused of being as old as Methuselah is just another way of saying that the individual has become overtaken by old age. According to the Holy Bible, the man called Methuselah lived to be 969 years old. Today's typical life span does not equate to 900 plus years, even if the measurement of time was different then. The concept is devoid of truth, and a definitive statement suggesting someone is as old as Methuselah is also devoid of truth.

CRACK THE WINDOW — Without giving any thought to what is being said, there is the frequent tendency of a person who wants a window opened slightly to let in a small amount of outside air, to say, "crack the window." It is understood that the intent is not to break a window pane to let in the air; nevertheless, the statement continues to be used over and over again.

I CAN'T WAIT — Hardly a day passes without someone making the statement, "I can't wait." This phrase suggests that the speaker cannot wait for something to happen. Although it may be hours, days, weeks, months, or even years before the event is to take place, the expression is still freely used, without concern. What will the person do other than wait, during the intervening time? For example, an engaged couple is to be married four months after one of the two makes the statement, "I can't wait until our wedding day." What happens during that four months? Are they not waiting? Or consider the college senior who is to graduate in June, who says in April, "I can't wait until I get my degree." If the student really could not wait, the degree would have been conferred in April. Of course, an infinite number of examples could be cited, but the fact is that the expression is usually just plain false. My father had a great deal of patience and would understand that this type of statement represents a state of anxiety, not a statement of truth.

GRAB THE BULL BY THE HORNS — If one is to be aggressive in pursuing a goal without showing hesitation or timidity, that person may be told to "grab the bull by the horns." In looking realistically at the boldness required for one to grab a bull by the horns, the aggressor is being advised to forget safety and do whatever is necessary to achieve the goal. The likelihood of literally carrying out this admonition is very slim. Even matadors, who fight bulls, do not grab them by the horns. The same reaction is forthcoming for those who suggest that we "grab the tiger by the tail."

HE PUT HIS FOOT IN HIS MOUTH — Should one say the wrong thing, it is not uncommon for another to say that, "he put his foot in his mouth." Although there is no physical contact between the foot and the mouth, the person who uttered the wrongful statement has little problem understanding the meaning of the charge. To put one's foot in one's mouth requires a level of agility and osteopathic elasticity that few people can claim.

I WAS A BASKET CASE — If a five-year-old child were told by a parent that, "I was a basket case," the child would have a tough, if not impossible, time understanding what the parent meant. Although the child's behavior might have contributed to the parent's state of being, there would still be no reference or basis from which the child could determine what the parent was talking about. The parent was trying to convey the message that he or she was so upset with something or somebody that both the physical and mental ability to function had been lost. The real meaning of the statement is that the parent had reached a state of death and had to be put in a basket and delivered to a funeral home by an undertaker. It is questionable whether this is really a sensible saying that makes no sense, or whether it is just a statement of nonsense.

I SLEPT LIKE A LOG - If one were to enjoy a restful night's sleep, he or she might express this by the phrase, "I slept like a log." After sleeping like a log, did the individual awaken like a log? The implication of the phrase is that logs are living creatures—which they are not. It is always heartening to learn that a person has experienced a good period of peaceful sleep, but it makes no sense to compare and equate that good sleep with that of a log (no longer part of a living entity) cut from a tree.

YOU ARE THE APPLE OF MY EYE - Admiration for another person can be expressed in many ways. This phrase indicates a feeling of love and affection for another. The problem with this expression, however, is that it suggests an anatomically incorrect or physically impossible characteristic of the human eye. If the statement had been made that, "You are the pupil of my eye," or "You are the retina of my eye," it would make more sense. To describe one as an apple of another person's eye makes no sense. It is hard to perceive an apple as part of one's eye.

TIME IS MOVING TOO FAST (SLOW) - As we grow older, we sometimes feel that the rate of time movement changes. This feeling usually arises from one of two different situations. One such situation is that the busier we get, the more things we attempt to do in the same amount of time when we were less busy. As a consequence, trying to do more things in an hour, in a day, in a week, a month, or in a year than we previously were able to do in a similar period of time, creates the false impression that time is not production friendly. On the other hand, if we find ourselves with fewer things to do than had previously been the case, we may feel that time is moving too slowly. As we know, time moves at the rate of sixty seconds per minute, sixty minutes per hour, and twenty-four hours per day. The length of the basic element of time, the second, is constant. Though it is possible to create certain scientific situations where time is not a critical factor, time itself goes through no unitary or rate change. To say that "time moves too fast or too slow" is not a statement based upon scientific fact.

IT'S RAINING CATS AND DOGS - One could possibly transport a planeload of cats and dogs above the ground and drop them in such a way that it would appear that it was raining cats and dogs. The same thing could be done with a rocket ship loaded with cats and dogs that are then released into the atmosphere. These are unlikely situations, but they could happen. "It's raining cats and dogs," of course refers to a downpour of falling rain water. This odd statement not only makes no sense, but is also highly confusing, bordering on fantasy.

HE DRIVES ME UP THE WALL - Can one be driven up a wall in a taxi or other vehicle? Hardly! How common it is for one person to say about another person, "He drives me up the wall." Imagine someone learning English attempting to comprehend the meaning of this phrase. The one who utters the saying is not happy with something that the target individual has either done or said. Whatever it might have been, it irritated the speaker and he/she chose to feel resentment. Perhaps the creator of the comic strip character of Spider-Man, was inspired by the saying even to the extent that the man who crawled up walls was born? I suppose that if anyone could drive someone up a wall, it would be Spider-Man, since he is the wall crawler.

LEAVE NO STONE UNTURNED - My father always pushed to explore various avenues to solve a problem, but the phrase, "leave no stone unturned," would not have been his comment. Yet this phrase is used in many cases when the person (or persons) involved is working on bringing a situation to a successful conclusion. Despite the fact that stones, more than likely, were not a relevant part of the activity, the information is still appreciated by the participants. Of course, the advisor is saying that every possible aspect or contributing factor relating to the situation that can be identified, should be examined to determine its effect upon the matter. This action should reveal what might otherwise be hidden flaws, hopefully making it easier to succeed than it would be if these flaws were not known. What makes no sense is the reference to turning stones.

ALL THE WAY AROUND ROBIN HOOD'S BARN - This phrase alludes to taking an obscure route to a planned destination. Although Robin Hood was a celebrated, traditional outlaw of the Twelfth Century, who lived with his followers in Sherwood Forest and robbed the rich to help the poor, it is questionable whether or not he owned a barn. Even if he did, the statement, while imaginative, lacks even fundamental accuracy. Yet, I think I went all around Robin Hood's barn to get to the end of this section that you are reading.

THE GOOD OLD DAYS ARE YET TO COME

My father never attempted to convince anyone that life had reached a point of maximum return. He talked more about what would happen than what had already happened. He often referred to what he termed "the good old days," but he did it in a futuristic way, as opposed to speaking of the past. Whenever he broached the subject of the "good old days," it was connected to his sincere feeling that life had more to offer than that which he and his family had experienced so far. Indeed, he tried to instill in the minds of his children that they were to strive to create for themselves a better life and time that could eventually be called "the good old days." In other words, he did not want his children to be satisfied with any accomplishment they might achieve or consider the accomplishment to be the ultimate achievement. Even if one thought that the zenith of life had been reached, my father wanted us to know that there was still far more to which we could and should aspire.

His message was well received by his children, for none of us ever succumbed to the practice of complacency. All of us look for the days that we can consider as "the good old days," but we refuse to allow ourselves to identify such days yet, because we are convinced that the best is never experienced until everything in life has been experienced. My father knew what he was talking about when he told us that "the good old days" really are yet to come.

In his own search for a time that he might look back upon as "the good old days," my father placed himself in a dream world.

NEVER STOP DREAMING

If ever a dreamer lived on this earth, it was he. There were times when he would tell stories to my brothers and sisters and me about dreams that bordered on fantasy. He would tell stories about how he had changed the entire world because he was in such close touch with God. He would talk about the great riches that one day he would inherit. He would talk about the great monetary riches he had already accumulated. He would tell us that he had so much money in the bank, that affixing his signature to any piece of paper on which a dollar amount had been advanced was sufficient authorization for the paper to be cashed as though it were a cashier's check. His favorite piece of paper on which to write one of his famous checks was that of a paper bag. If he should sign the paper bag with a dollar amount on it, the bank would honor it without question and put the money in the bag. His signature was so powerful, he would say, that he had to be extremely careful about where it appeared. In other words, he considered his signature to be, in effect, a blank check for anyone fortunate enough to get it.

His dreaming not only involved power, money and riches, but it also was associated with such things as fishing and hunting. Stories about fish so large that they broke his lines and swam away were quite common. For some reason, he always thought that he could catch fish as large as the body of a man and then use them for feeding many people. These were always the fish that got away, but he had seen them and insisted that they were real.

As far as hunting game animals is concerned, he created unbelievable stories about seeing deer, huge rabbits and squirrels, and quail so large that his guns were just not powerful enough to stop them. In fact, there were many times, he claimed, that he had to seek places of safety to keep from being devoured by the animals. His dream was to be able, one day, to develop the means to capture these animals and use them for food. That day never came. In all likelihood, the sharing of such dreams with his children was a conscious effort on his part to teach them that life, if it is to be meaningful, must include not only the ability to dream, but also the recognized necessity for dreaming, for the reality of tomorrow is based upon today's dream. Tomorrow can only be experienced if it exists in today's dream. The fundamental precept of my father's dream was that one day he and his loved ones would live in comfort and security in the world created by his dreams. He never abandoned the notion that this great day would come. He believed and he taught that to dream is to eat the sustaining food of life, however farfetched that dream may be. Without dreams, there is an emptiness that will never be filled.

At the time of my father's burial, vivid thoughts of his dreaming came to my mind. As my family and many of our friends were about to leave the cemetery, my eyes were focused on the beautiful flowers adorning his grave site, as a brilliant sun shone upon it. The beauty of the setting was such that I concluded that he had found real truth in his dreams in the form of peace and tranquillity. He would never again have to fantasize about what would or should be.

I decided, as we drove away, that he had now realized what one of our great philosophers had written, "The best thing in this life is the search for a better life." My father had finally achieved his dream—a better life.

Owen Douglas Nichols

From the beginning, Dr. Nichols has been a scholar, always seeking to gather and disseminate knowledge.

Born in Raleigh, North Carolina, he was valedictorian for both his Washington High School graduation class of 1948, and for his Shaw University class of 1955. At Shaw, he received a Bachelor of Science degree in chemistry. In 1958, he received a Master's Degree in chemistry from Howard University, Washington, DC. He was awarded the Doctor of Education degree in education administration and supervision from Highland University in Maryville, Tennessee, in 1975.

Dr. Nichols has brought his scholarship to bear both in the professional areas of his discipline, and in his outstanding community service. From 1950 to 1953, he served as a commissioned officer in the United States Army Corps of Engineers. Besides active military duty, his government service included that of research chemist with the U.S. Naval Research Laboratory and physical science analyst with the Department of Defense from 1962 to 1966.

Dr. Nichols began his distinguished academic career as an associate professor of chemistry at South Carolina State College in Orangeburg in 1958. He moved to Howard University in 1969 as the Executive Assistant to the President. When he retired from nearly 20 years of service at Howard University in 1988, he had served for 17 years as Vice President for Administration and as Secretary of the University and as Secretary of the Board of Trustees.

During his tenure at Howard, Dr. Nichols was instrumental in the development and executive oversight of WHUR-FM, WHMM-TV (Channel 32), and the University's Office of Satellite Communications. These electronic media helped set Howard University apart as one of the nation's most progressive and comprehensive Institutions of higher learning.

Over the years, local communities in Prince George's and Montgomery counties have benefited from Dr. Nichols' scholarly service to young people and their supportive organizations. Outstanding among these has been his development and leadership of the African American Festival of Academic Excellence. He also has served as Sunday School Superintendent and Trustee of Sergeant Memorial Presbyterian Church in Washington, DC.

Dr. Nichols is currently a member of the Board of Trustees of Montgomery College.

Dr. Nichols and his wife, Delores, are proud parents of Bryan Keesee Nichols and Diane Maria Nichols.